FAVORITE RECIPES® PRESENTS

Kitchen Auditions

A Cookbook for Bands and Cheering Squads

© Favorite Recipes Press MCMLXXVI
Post Office Box 3396, Montgomery, Alabama 36109

Library of Congress Cataloging in Publication Data
Main entry under title:

Favorite Recipes presents kitchen auditions, a cookbook
for bands and cheering squads.

Includes index.
1. Cookery. I. Title: Kitchen auditions.
TX715.F27798   641.5   76-21087
ISBN 0-87197-105-4

DEAR PATRON . . .

May I present this Cookbook as a salute to the thousands of generous parents and friends who contribute annually to their local School Bands and Cheering Squads . . . it has been designed to reflect the free and lively spirit as well as the youthful exuberance of this age.

Occasionally we lose track of these important school activities, Bands and Pep Squads, as we attend the necessities of everyday life, but we would all agree the sound of a School Band or Cheering Squad is a nostalgic and thrilling reminder of an important aspect of life to every American.

This Cookbook will serve as a useful and lasting reminder that you gave your support and contributed to a very worthwhile endeavor . . . the continuing success of your School Band and Cheering Squad. Remember the importance of both groups; they are a part of our heritage as well as our all-time pleasure.

Sincerely,

Nicky Beaulieu

Nicky Beaulieu
Associate Editor

BOARD OF ADVISORS

Earl Dunn
Muncie, Indiana
School of Music, Ball State University
Past President, National Band Association

Earl Dunn

George S. Howard, USAF Col. (RET)
San Antonio, Texas
Former Director, United States Air Force Band
Past President, American Band Masters
   Association

George S. Howard

William Ledue
Coral Gables, Florida
President, Florida Music Educators Association

Bill Ledue

Bill Sloan
Huntsville, Alabama
President, Alabama Band Association

Bill Sloan

Contents

Substitutions and Cooking Guides

WHEN YOU'RE MISSING AN INGREDIENT...

Substitute 1 teaspoon dried herbs for 1 tablespoon fresh herbs.

Add 1/4 teaspoon baking soda and 1/2 cup buttermilk to equal 1 teaspoon baking powder. The buttermilk will replace 1/2 cup of the liquid indicated in the recipe.

Use 3 tablespoons dry cocoa plus 1 tablespoon butter or margarine instead of 1 square (1 ounce) unsweetened chocolate.

Make custard with 1 whole egg rather than 2 egg yolks.

Mix 1/2 cup evaporated milk with 1/2 cup water (or 1 cup reconstituted nonfat dry milk with 1 tablespoon butter) to replace 1 cup whole milk.

Make 1 cup of sour milk by letting stand for 5 minutes 1 tablespoon lemon juice or vinegar plus sweet milk to make 1 cup.

Substitute 1 package (2 teaspoons) active dry yeast for 1 cake compressed yeast.

Add 1 tablespoon instant minced onion, rehydrated, to replace 1 small fresh onion.

Substitute 1 tablespoon prepared mustard for 1 teaspoon dry mustard.

Use 1/8 teaspoon garlic powder instead of 1 small pressed clove of garlic.

Substitute 2 tablespoons of flour for 1 tablespoon of cornstarch to use as a thickening agent.

Mix 1/2 cup tomato sauce with 1/2 cup of water to make 1 cup tomato juice.

Make catsup or chili with 1 cup tomato sauce plus 1/2 cup sugar and 2 tablespoons vinegar.

CAN SIZE CHART

8 oz. can or jar	1 c.	1 lb. 4 oz. or 1 pt. 2 fl. oz. or No. 2 can or jar	2 1/2 c.
10 1/2 oz. can (picnic can)	1 1/4 c.	1 lb. 13 oz. can or jar or No. 2 1/2 can or jar	3 1/2 c.
12 oz. can (vacuum)	1 1/2 c.	1 qt. 14 fl. oz. or 3 lb. 3 oz. or 46 oz. can	5 3/4 c.
14-16 oz. or No. 300 can	1 1/4 c.	6 1/2 to 7 1/2 lb. or No. 10 can	12-13 c.
16-17 oz. can or jar or No. 303 can or jar	2 c.		

SUBSTITUTIONS

1 square *chocolate* (1 ounce) = 3 or 4 tablespoons cocoa plus 1/2 tablespoon fat.

1 tablespoon *cornstarch* (for thickening) = 2 tablespoons flour (approximately).

1 cup sifted *all-purpose flour* = 1 cup plus 2 tablespoons sifted cake flour.

1 cup sifted *cake flour* = 1 cup minus 2 tablespoons sifted all-purpose flour.

1 teaspoon *baking powder* = 1/4 teaspoon baking soda plus 1/2 teaspoon cream of tartar.

1 cup *bottled milk* = 1/2 cup evaporated milk plus 1/2 cup water.

1 cup *sour milk* = 1 cup sweet milk into which 1 tablespoon vinegar or lemon juice has been stirred; or 1 cup buttermilk.

1 cup *sweet milk* = 1 cup sour milk or buttermilk plus 1/2 teaspoon baking soda.

1 cup *canned tomatoes* = about 1 1/3 cups cut-up fresh tomatoes, simmered 10 minutes.

3/4 cup *cracker crumbs* = 1 cup bread crumbs.

1 cup *cream, sour, heavy* = 1/3 cup butter and 2/3 cup milk in any sour milk recipe.

1 cup *cream, sour, thin* = 3 tablespoons butter and 3/4 cup milk in sour milk recipe.

1 cup *molasses* = 1 cup honey.

Metric Conversion Chart

VOLUME

1 tsp.	=	4.9 cc
1 tbsp.	=	14.7 cc
1/3 c.	=	28.9 cc
1/8 c.	=	29.5 cc
1/4 c.	=	59.1 cc
1/2 c.	=	118.3 cc
3/4 c.	=	177.5 cc
1 c.	=	236.7 cc
2 c.	=	473.4 cc
1 fl. oz.	=	29.5 cc
4 oz.	=	118.3 cc
8 oz.	=	236.7 cc

1 pt.	=	473.4 cc
1 qt.	=	.946 liters
1 gal.	=	3.7 liters

CONVERSION FACTORS:

Liters	X	1.056	=	Liquid quarts
Quarts	X	0.946	=	Liters
Liters	X	0.264	=	Gallons
Gallons	X	3.785	=	Liters
Fluid ounces	X	29.563	=	Cubic centimeters
Cubic centimeters	X	0.034	=	Fluid ounces
Cups	X	236.575	=	Cubic centimeters
Tablespoons	X	14.797	=	Cubic centimeters
Teaspoons	X	4.932	=	Cubic centimeters
Bushels	X	0.352	=	Hectoliters
Hectoliters	X	2.837	=	Bushels

WEIGHT

1 dry oz.	=	28.3 Grams
1 lb.	=	.454 Kilograms

CONVERSION FACTORS:

Ounces (Avoir.)	X	28.349	=	Grams
Grams	X	0.035	=	Ounces
Pounds	X	0.454	=	Kilograms
Kilograms	X	2.205	=	Pounds

Equivalent Chart

3 tsp. = 1 tbsp.
2 tbsp. = 1/8 c.
4 tbsp. = 1/4 c.
8 tbsp. = 1/2 c.
16 tbsp. = 1 c.
5 tbsp. + 1 tsp. = 1/3 c.
12 tbsp. = 3/4 c.
4 oz. = 1/2 c.
8 oz. = 1 c.

16 oz. = 1 lb.
1 oz. = 2 tbsp. fat or liquid
2 c. fat = 1 lb.
2 c. = 1 pt.
2 c. sugar = 1 lb.
5/8 c. = 1/2 c. + 2 tbsp.
7/8 c. = 3/4 c. + 2 tbsp.
2 2/3 c. powdered sugar = 1 lb.
2 2/3 c. brown sugar = 1 lb.

4 c. sifted flour = 1 lb.
1 lb. butter = 2 c. or 4 sticks
2 pt. = 1 qt.
1 qt. = 4 c.
A Few Grains = Less than 1/8 tsp.
Pinch is as much as can be taken between tip of finger and thumb.
Speck = Less than 1/8 tsp.

WHEN YOU NEED APPROXIMATE MEASUREMENTS . . .

1 lemon makes 3 tablespoons juice
1 lemon makes 1 teaspoon grated peel
1 orange makes 1/3 cup juice
1 orange makes about 2 teaspoons grated peel
1 chopped medium onion makes 1/2 cup pieces
1 pound unshelled walnuts makes 1 1/2 to 1 3/4 cups shelled
1 pound unshelled almonds makes 3/4 to 1 cup shelled
8 to 10 egg whites make 1 cup

12 to 14 egg yolks make 1 cup
1 pound shredded American cheese makes 4 cups
1/4 pound crumbled blue cheese makes 1 cup
1 cup unwhipped cream makes 2 cups whipped
4 ounces (1 to 1 1/4 cups) uncooked macaroni makes 2 1/4 cups cooked
7 ounces spaghetti make 4 cups cooked
4 ounces (1 1/2 to 2 cups) uncooked noodles make 2 cups cooked.

MAKE 1 CUP OF FINE CRUMBS WITH . . .

28 saltine crackers
4 slices bread
14 square graham crackers
22 vanilla wafers

Candy Test

TYPE OF CANDY	COLD WATER TEST	TEMPERATURE AT SEA LEVEL* (in degrees as measured on candy thermometer)
Fudge, fondant	Soft-ball stage (flattens when picked up)	234-240°
Caramels	Firm-ball stage (holds shape unless pressed)	240-248°
Divinity, taffy	Hard-ball stage (holds shape but is still pliable)	250-268°
Butterscotch, English toffee	Soft-crack stage (separates into hard threads that are not brittle)	270-290°
Brittles	Hard-crack stage (separates into hard threads that crack when pressed between fingers)	300-310°

*Subtract approximately two degrees for every 1,000 feet increase in altitude.

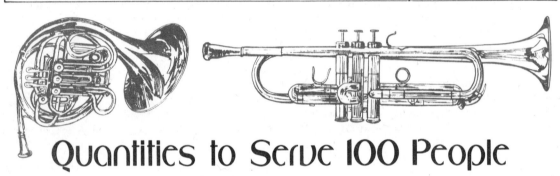

Quantities to Serve 100 People

Baked beans . . . . .5 gallons	Loaf sugar . . . . 3 pounds
Beef . . . . 40 pounds	Meat loaf . . . . 24 pounds
Beets . . . . 30 pounds	Milk . . . . .6 gallons
Bread . . . . 10 loaves	Nuts . . . . 3 pounds
Butter . . . . 3 pounds	Olives . . . . 1 3/4 pounds
Cabbage for slaw . . . . 20 pounds	Oysters . . . . 18 quarts
Cakes . . . . .8 cakes	Pickles . . . . 2 quarts
Carrots . . . . 33 pounds	Pies . . . . 18 pies
Cauliflower . . . . 18 pounds	Potatoes . . . . 35 pounds
Cheese . . . . 3 pounds	Potato salad . . . . 12 quarts
Chicken for chicken pie . . . . 40 pounds	Roast pork . . . . 40 pounds
Coffee . . . . 3 pounds	Rolls . . . . .200 rolls
Cream . . . . 3 quarts	Salad dressing . . . . 3 quarts
Fruit cocktail . . . . 1 gallon	Scalloped potatoes . . . . .5 gallons
Fruit juice . . . . 4 No. 10 cans	Soup . . . . .5 gallons
Fruit salad . . . . 20 quarts	Tomato juice . . . . 4 No. 10 cans
Ham . . . . 40 pounds	Vegetables . . . . 4 No. 10 cans
Hamburger . . . . .30 to 36 pounds	Vegetable salad . . . . 20 quarts
Ice Cream .4 gallons	Whipping cream . . . . 4 pints
Lettuce . . . . .20 heads	Wieners . . . . 25 pounds

Emergency First Aid

POISONING: When a poison has been taken internally, start first aid at once. Call doctor immediately.

1. Dilute poison with large amounts of liquids — milk, or water.
2. Wash out by inducing vomiting, when not a strong acid, strong alkali or petroleum.
3. For acid poisons do not induce vomiting, but neutralize with milk of magnesia. Then give milk, olive oil or egg white. Keep victim warm and lying down.
4. For alkali poisons such as lye or ammonia, do not induce vomiting; give lemon juice or vinegar. Then give milk and keep victim warm and lying down.
5. If poison is a sleeping drug, induce vomiting and then give strong black coffee frequently. Victim must be kept awake.
6. If breathing stops, give artificial respiration.

SHOCK: Shock is brought on by a sudden or severe physical injury or emotional disturbance. In shock, the balance between the nervous system and the blood vessels is upset. The result is faintness, nausea, and a pale and clammy skin. Call doctor immediately. If not treated the victim may become unconscious and eventually lapse into a coma.

1. Keep victim lying down.
2. Don't give fluids unless delayed in getting to doctor, then give only water. (Hot tea, coffee, milk or broth may be tried if water is not tolerated.)
3. Never give liquid to an unconscious person.
4. Cover victim both under and around his body.
5. Do not permit victim to become abnormally hot.
6. Reassure victim and avoid letting him see other victims, or his own injury.

FRACTURES: Pain, deformity or swelling of injured part usually means a fracture. If fracture is suspected, don't move person unless absolutely necessary, and then only if the suspected area is splinted. Give small amounts of lukewarm fluids and treat for shock.

BURNS: Apply or submerge the burned area in cold water. Apply a protective dry sterile cloth or gauze dry dressing if necessary. Do not apply grease or an antiseptic ointment or spray. Call doctor and keep patient with severe burns warm, not hot.

1. If burn case must be transported any distance, cover burns with clean cloth.
2. Don't dress extensive facial burns. (It may hinder early plastic surgery.)

WOUNDS: Minor Cuts: Apply pressure with sterile gauze until bleeding stops. Use antiseptic recommended by your doctor. Bandage with sterile gauze. See your doctor. **Puncture Wounds:** Cover with sterile gauze and consult doctor immediately. Serious infection can arise unless properly treated.

ANIMAL BITES: Wash wounds freely with soap and water. Hold under running tap for several minutes if possible. Apply an antiseptic approved by your doctor and cover with sterile gauze compress. Always see your doctor immediately. Obtain name and address of owner so that animal may be held in quarantine if necessary.

HEAT EXHAUSTION: Caused by exposure to heat or sun. **Symptoms:** Pale face, moist and clammy skin, weak pulse, subnormal temperature, victim is usually conscious. **Treatment:** Keep victim lying down; keep legs elevated; keep victim wrapped in blanket. Give ½ glass salt water to drink every 15 minutes (1 teaspoon salt to 1 glass water).

General Directions For First Aid

1. Effect a prompt rescue.
2. Maintain an open airway.
3. Control severe bleeding.
4. Give First Aid for poisoning.
5. Do not move victim unless it is necessary for safety reasons.
6. Protect the victim from unnecessary manipulation and disturbance.
7. Avoid or overcome chilling by using blankets or covers, if available.
8. Determine the injuries or cause for sudden illness.
9. Examine the victim methodically but be guided by the kind of accident or sudden illness and the need of the situation.
10. Carry out the indicated First Aid.

Jazzy Appetizers & Sauces

Thanks to the Unsinkable Molly Brown, America was introduced to the tasty treat of appetizers. She first experienced hors d'oeuvres at teatime on a cruise to London, and was immediately taken with the idea of serving finger foods before dinner to sharpen the appetite. Happily, she brought many delicious appetizer recipes home with her.

Appetizers, regardless of the occasion, can be prepared from the lowliest of leftovers, or the fanciest of gourmet specialties. Still, they are so simple to make! When the cheerleaders and the pep squad members meet to make plans for the next pep rally, *Pizzicato Pizzas* and *Sharps And Flats* will have everyone cheering. Then, at fund-raising committee meetings for the band, serve *Crowd-Pleasing Pickled Shrimp* and *Fiesta Hot Bean Dip*.

Band members and cheerleaders can make big batches of *Hot Fudge Sauce* to serve at home and at parties, with hardly any trouble and lots of enjoyment. Try any of these Jazzy Appetizers and Sauces — during the next meeting, after the big game, or any time at all! As every band member and cheerleader knows, you'll be glad you did.

CAROB NUGGET SNACK

1 c. bite-sized cereal
1/2 c. chow mein noodles
2 tsp. butter or margarine, melted
1 tsp. Worcestershire sauce
3 drops of Tabasco sauce
1/2 c. dried apricots
1/4 c. carob nuggets
1/2 c. salted peanuts, sunflower seed or
    pumpkin seed

Combine cereal and noodles in bowl. Mix butter, Worcestershire sauce and Tabasco sauce together. Pour over cereal mixture; mix well. Add remaining ingredients; toss lightly. Store in airtight container.

Photograph for this recipe on page 8.

BROILED CHICKEN LIVERS

Sliced bacon
Water chestnuts
Soy sauce
Chicken livers

Cut bacon strips in half; quarter chestnuts. Marinate bacon and chestnuts in soy sauce. Cut chicken livers in small pieces. Wrap 1 piece chicken liver and 1 piece chestnut with bacon strip; secure with toothpick. Broil until bacon is browned.

GOLDEN CHICKEN NUGGETS

2 sm. whole chicken breasts
1/2 c. corn flake crumbs
1 tsp. salt
1/4 tsp. pepper
1/4 c. melted butter

Skin and bone chicken; cut into 1-inch chunks. Combine corn flake crumbs, salt and pepper. Dip chicken into butter; roll in crumb mixture. Arrange chicken in single layer on foil-lined baking sheet. Bake in preheated 400-degree oven for 30 minutes or until golden brown.

MINUTEMAN MEATBALLS

1 lb. ground lean beef
1/2 c. fine bread crumbs

1/2 c. evaporated milk
1/4 c. minced onion
1/4 c. catsup or chili sauce
1 tbsp. Worcestershire sauce
1 tsp. salt
1 tsp. pepper
1 egg
2 to 3 tbsp. butter

Combine all ingredients except butter; mix well. Shape into small balls. Brown on all sides in butter, shaking skillet to keep balls round.

Dunky Sauce

1 8-oz. can tomato sauce
1/2 c. catsup
2 tbsp. minced onion
2 tbsp. pickle relish, drained
2 tbsp. water
1 tbsp. vinegar
2 tbsp. Worcestershire sauce
1 or 2 drops of hot sauce
Pepper to taste

Combine all ingredients in saucepan; bring to a boil. Pour into fondue pot. Spear meatballs with fondue forks or skewers; dip into sauce.

FRANKFURTER FANFARE

1/2 c. prepared mustard
1 c. apple or currant jelly
1 lb. frankfurters

Combine mustard and jelly in chafing dish or double boiler. Slice frankfurters diagonally into bite-sized pieces; add to sauce. Heat thoroughly.

SUPER SAUSAGE BITES

3 c. biscuit mix
1 8-oz. package sharp cheese, grated
1 lb. highly seasoned bulk sausage

Combine biscuit mix, cheese and sausage; blend well. Roll sausage mixture into small balls; place on baking sheets. Bake in preheated 425-degree oven for 10 minutes or until browned. Serve hot. Yield: 20 servings.

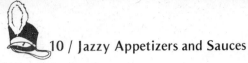

PIZZICATO PIZZAS

1 lb. hamburger
3 tbsp. minced onions
Salt and pepper to taste
1 6-oz. can tomato paste
1 tsp. Worcestershire sauce
1/2 tsp. oregano
2 cans oven-ready biscuits
1/2 lb. grated mozzarella cheese

Saute hamburger and onions until lightly browned; drain off excess fat. Season with salt and pepper. Combine tomato paste, Worcestershire sauce and oregano; heat to boiling point. Flatten biscuits into 3-inch circles. Spread with hamburger mixture; cover with sauce. Top with cheese. Bake in preheated 425-degree oven for 10 minutes. Yield: 20 small pizzas.

TUNA CHILI CON QUESO

1 tbsp. butter or margarine
1/4 c. chopped onion
1 1-lb. can tomatoes, drained and chopped
1 bay leaf
2 tbsp. flour
1/4 c. milk
1 4-oz. can green chilies, drained, seeded and chopped
1/4 tsp. salt
1 c. shredded Monterey Jack or Cheddar cheese
1 7-oz. can tuna

Melt butter in saucepan. Add onion; saute until tender. Add tomatoes and bay leaf; simmer for 5 minutes, stirring occasionally. Combine flour and milk to make a paste. Stir into tomato mixture; simmer for 5 minutes. Remove bay leaf. Add green chilies, salt and cheese; stir until cheese melts. Stir in tuna. Keep warm; serve with corn chips, if desired. Yield: 2 cups.

Photograph for this recipe on page 17.

TUNA CHEESE BALLS

1 7-oz. can tuna
1 8-oz. package farmer cheese, grated
1/4 c. chopped parsley

2 tsp. grated onion
4 tsp. lemon juice
2 tsp. Worcestershire sauce
1 2-oz. can chopped mushrooms, drained

Drain tuna; place in bowl. Break into fine flakes. Add remaining ingredients; mix well. Shape into 1-inch balls. Chill thoroughly. May serve plain or roll in chopped dried beef, sesame seed, chopped parsley or chopped nuts. Yield: About 3 dozen balls.

Photograph for this recipe on page 17.

CHEESE SHARP DELIGHTS

1 lb. sharp Cheddar cheese, grated
1 1/2 c. butter or margarine, softened
4 c. all-purpose flour
1 tsp. salt
1/2 tsp. cayenne pepper

Combine cheese and butter; cream until well blended. Sift flour, salt and pepper together; blend into butter mixture. Shape into rolls, 1 1/2 inches in diameter. Wrap in waxed paper; refrigerate overnight. Slice 1/4 inch thick; place on baking sheet. Bake in preheated 425-degree oven until edges are lightly browned.

Chill cheese to grate it more easily.

HIGH NOTE NACHOS

1 pkg. Doritos or tortillas, cut into eights
1 sm. package Cheddar cheese or jalapeno cheese
1 4-oz. can chopped green chilies

Place Doritos on cookie sheet; grate cheese over top of chips. Place chilies on each chip. Bake in preheated 400-degree oven until cheese melts.

TOASTED CHEESE ROUNDS

1/3 c. grated Parmesan cheese
3/4 c. mayonnaise
1/4 c. finely chopped onion
Dash of Worcestershire sauce

Salt and pepper to taste
1 loaf party rye bread

Combine cheese, mayonnaise, onion, Worcestershire sauce, salt and pepper; blend well. Spread cheese mixture on bread slices, then place on baking sheets. Broil 3 to 4 inches from source of heat for 2 to 3 minutes or until lightly browned. Serve immediately.

BROILED OLIVES

1/2 pkg. sliced bacon
1 jar lg. olives

Cut bacon slices in half. Wrap each olive in bacon slice; secure with wooden pick. Broil 5 inches from source of heat until bacon is crisp; turn to broil evenly.

SHARPS AND FLATS

3/4 c. butter or margarine
1 tbsp. Worcestershire sauce
1 tsp. celery salt
1 tsp. salt
1/2 tsp. garlic salt
1 box Wheat Chex
1 box Rice Chex
1 box pretzels
1 box Cheerios
1 can mixed nuts

Combine first 5 ingredients in saucepan; heat, stirring, until butter is melted. Place remaining ingredients in roasting pan. Pour butter mixture over cereal mixture; toss to mix well. Bake in preheated 250-degree oven for 1 hour, stirring every 10 minutes.

CLASSIC CHEESE FONDUE

1 garlic clove, split
1/2 lb. Swiss cheese, grated
1/2 lb. Gruyere cheese, grated
3 tbsp. flour
2 c. dry white wine
Dash of nutmeg
French or Italian bread, cut in 1-in. cubes

Rub side and bottom of fondue pot with garlic. Mix cheeses; sprinkle with flour. Pour wine into fondue pot; place over low heat until bubbles rise. Do not boil. Add cheese, one handful at a time, stirring constantly with a wooden spoon until the cheese is melted and smooth. Stir in nutmeg. Keep fondue bubbling while serving. Spear bread on fondue forks; swirl in figure 8 motion in cheese mixture. Yield: 8-10 servings.

DIP AND CRUNCH

1 3-oz. package cream cheese
1/2 c. mayonnaise
3 tbsp. catsup

Place cream cheese in mixing bowl; let stand to room temperature. Stir in mayonnaise and catsup; mix well. Serve as dip with fresh carrot slices, lettuce, cauliflowerets, cherry tomatoes and celery pieces, if desired. Yield: 1 cup dip.

Photograph for this recipe on page 18.

DAFFODIL DIP FOR VEGETABLES

1/2 c. mayonnaise
1 8-oz. package cream cheese, softened
1/2 c. minced parsley
1 hard-boiled egg
2 tbsp. chopped onion
1 garlic clove, pressed
1 tbsp. anchovy paste
Dash of pepper

Add mayonnaise to cream cheese gradually, blending well after each addition. Add parsley, finely chopped egg white, onion, garlic, anchovy paste and pepper; mix well. Sprinkle sieved egg yolk over dip. Serve with fresh vegetables. Yield: 2 1/2 cups.

FIESTA HOT BEAN DIP

2 cans refried beans
2 tbsp. chopped jalapeno peppers
1/2 tsp. liquid from peppers
1 tsp. Worcestershire sauce
6 tbsp. melted margarine
Onion salt and garlic salt to taste

Combine all ingredients; heat thoroughly. Serve with corn chips, crackers or tostados. Yield: 12-16 servings.

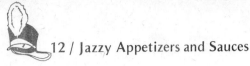

CHARLIE'S TUNA-ONION DIP

1   7-oz. can tuna
1 pkg. dry onion soup mix
1 c. sour cream
1/4 c. Chablis

Drain tuna; flake. Combine all ingredients; mix well. Chill for at least 1 hour. Serve as dip with crackers, potato chips or fresh vegetable sticks.

CURRIED TUNA DIP

1   7-oz. can tuna
1/2 c. chopped onion
1/2 c. chopped pared apple
1 tsp. curry powder
1 c. creamed cottage cheese
1 tbsp. milk
1 tsp. lemon juice
1/4 tsp. salt

Drain oil from tuna into skillet. Saute onion, apple and curry powder in hot oil until onion and apple are tender. Turn into electric blender container. Add cottage cheese, milk, lemon juice and salt; process at high speed until smooth. Flake tuna in bowl. Add cottage cheese mixture; mix well. Chill thoroughly. Serve as dip with fresh celery pieces, broccoli flowerets, sliced carrots, cherry tomatoes and cucumber slices, if desired. Yield: 1 1/2 cups.

Photograph for this recipe on page 17.

ZINGY AVOCADO DIP

4 fully ripe avocados
1/2 c. mayonnaise
1/4 c. minced onion
Salt to taste
2 tsp. chili powder
1 tsp. garlic powder
1/2 tsp. Tabasco sauce
3 tbsp. lemon juice
2 med. tomatoes, peeled and chopped

Cut avocados in half lengthwise, twisting gently to separate halves. Whack a sharp knife directly into seeds and twist to lift out. Peel avocados, then mash pulp until smooth. Mix with mayonnaise, onion, seasonings and lemon juice. Stir in tomatoes. Chill thoroughly before serving.

CROWD-PLEASING PICKLED SHRIMP

1/2 c. crab boil
3 1/2 tsp. salt
1 bay leaf
2 1/2 lb. shrimp
1 c. salad oil
2 1/2 tsp. celery seed
2 1/2 tsp. capers
3/4 c. white vinegar
1 tsp. salt
Dash of Tabasco sauce
2 lg. onions, sliced
1 jar green and black olives

Combine 6 cups water, crab boil, salt and bay leaf in large kettle; bring to a boil. Add shrimp; cook for about 10 minutes or until shrimp turn pink. Combine salad oil, celery seed, capers, vinegar, salt and Tabasco; mix well. Drain shrimp; shell and devein. Arrange alternate layers of shrimp, onions and olives in container with tight-fitting lid. Pour marinade over all. Refrigerate for 24 hours, turning container occasionally so all shrimp are marinated. Yield: 10-12 servings.

BUTTERSCOTCH ICE CREAM SAUCE

1 1/2 c. (packed) brown sugar
1/4 c. butter
2/3 c. white corn syrup
3/4 c. evaporated milk

Combine brown sugar, butter and corn syrup in heavy saucepan over medium heat; stir until butter is melted and ingredients are blended. Bring to a boil; cook to soft-ball stage or 235 degrees on candy thermometer. Remove from heat; cool slightly. Add evaporated milk slowly, stirring until blended. Store in refrigerator. Serve over ice cream.

EASY PINEAPPLE SAUCE

1 c. orange juice
2 tbsp. lemon juice
1 sm. can crushed pineapple
Dash of salt
1/2 c. sugar
4 tbsp. cornstarch
6 tbsp. butter

Combine juices, pineapple, salt and sugar; mix well. Combine 1/2 cup water and cornstarch; stir into pineapple mixture. Bring to a boil; simmer, stirring constantly, for 5 minutes. Remove from heat; stir in butter. Serve on sliced angel food or pound cake.

HOT FUDGE SAUCE

1/2 c. butter, softened
2 1/4 c. powdered sugar
2/3 c. evaporated milk
6 sq. semisweet chocolate

Combine butter and sugar in top of double boiler. Stir in evaporated milk; add chocolate. Cook over hot water for 30 minutes. Do not stir. Remove from heat; beat until creamy. Store in refrigerator and reheat as needed. Add cream for a thinner sauce. Yield: 1 1/2 pints.

HE-MAN BARBECUE SAUCE

1 c. catsup
3 tbsp. Worcestershire sauce
2 or 3 dashes of Tabasco sauce
1 c. water
1/4 c. vinegar
1 tbsp. sugar
1 tsp. salt
1 tsp. celery seed

Combine all ingredients in saucepan; bring to a boil. Simmer for 30 minutes. Excellent sauce for barbecued ribs.

MARINADE FOR BEEF

1 c. salad oil
1/2 c. vinegar
1 clove of garlic, split
2 tsp. Worcestershire sauce
1 tsp. salt
1/4 tsp. pepper
Dash of cayenne pepper
Dash of Tabasco sauce
2 tsp. dry mustard

Combine all ingredients in jar; shake well. Remove garlic. Pour marinade over beef; marinate for at least 3 hours.

SEAFOOD COCKTAIL SAUCE

3/4 c. chili sauce
1/4 c. lemon juice
2 tsp. Worcestershire sauce
1/2 tsp. grated onion
4 drops of Tabasco sauce
Salt to taste

Combine all ingredients; mix well. Chill thoroughly.

TARTAR SAUCE SUPREME

1 c. mayonnaise
1 1/2 tbsp. minced pickles
1 1/2 tbsp. minced parsley
1 1/2 tbsp. capers
1 1/2 tbsp. grated onion
1 1/2 tbsp. minced green olives

Combine all ingredients in a bowl; chill for several hours before using.

Sousa's Soups & Sandwiches

What goes together like bands and music, majorettes and batons and cheerleaders and pompons? Soups and sandwiches, of course!!! They team to make one of the quickest, easiest and most nourishing meals possible for girls and boys on-the-go. And, because there are so many varieties of soups and sandwiches, your family can enjoy them often.

Just as John Philip Sousa, one of the most famous of all American bandmasters and composers, was constantly striving to produce music of the highest quality, you are constantly looking for new ways to serve your family the very best meals possible. Sousa's Soups and Sandwiches can help you do just that.

Since most of these recipes are so simple to prepare, even the younger set can enjoy their turn in the kitchen. Let them try *Lettermen's Club Sandwiches, Ragtime Ragout* or *Go-For-Two Tuna Sandwiches* after band practice, before the game . . . . anytime! Whatever the occasion, there is sure to be a soup and sandwich recipe here that is just right!

QUICK AND EASY CHICKEN-MUSHROOM SOUP

1 can cream of mushroom soup
1 can chicken broth
2 c. water
2 tbsp. butter
1 tsp. salt
1 can boned chicken, chopped
1 tbsp. chopped chives
1 tsp. curry powder (opt.)
1 c. cream
1 c. cooked rice

Combine all ingredients in large saucepan; heat through.

HOMEMADE CHICKEN-NOODLE SOUP

1 frying chicken, disjointed
1 carrot, diced
1 stalk celery, diced
1 onion, diced
3 peppercorns
2 chicken bouillon cubes
1 tbsp. salt
Juice of 1/2 lemon
1 pkg. fine noodles

Place chicken in large kettle; add carrot, celery, onion, peppercorns, bouillon cubes, salt, lemon juice and 2 quarts water. Bring to a boil; reduce heat. Cover; simmer until chicken is tender. Remove chicken from broth; cool. Remove chicken from bones; add to soup. Break noodles into 1-inch pieces; add to soup. Cook for 15 minutes longer or until noodles are done. Remove peppercorns; serve. Yield: 6 servings.

CREAM OF CELERY SOUP

2 c. chopped celery
1/2 c. butter
1/2 c. flour
2 qt. chicken stock or bouillon
2 or 3 celery tops
1 c. light cream
1/2 tsp. chervil
1/4 tsp. white pepper
Dash of nutmeg
2 tsp. grated onion

Salt to taste
Chopped parsley to taste

Cook celery in butter in saucepan over low heat until crisp-tender; stir in flour. Add 1 quart stock gradually; add celery tops. Cook, stirring, until mixture comes to a boil; boil for 1 minute. Discard celery tops. Place sauce in blender container; cover. Process for 1 minute; return to saucepan. Stir in remaining 1 quart stock, cream and remaining ingredients; bring just to a boil. Yield: 10-12 servings.

EASY ONION SOUP

1/4 c. butter
1 lb. yellow onions, minced
2 tbsp. flour
4 c. water
5 beef bouillon cubes
1/2 tsp. salt
6 thin slices French bread
1/2 c. grated Parmesan cheese

Melt butter in heavy saucepan. Add onions and flour; cook for 15 minutes or until golden brown. Add water, bouillon cubes and salt; bring to a boil, stirring until bouillon cubes are dissolved. Cover tightly; reduce heat. Simmer for 15 minutes. Toast bread until golden brown; place 1 slice in bottom of each of 6 soup bowls. Ladle soup over bread; sprinkle with cheese. Yield: 6 servings.

GAZPACHO GRANDE

1 c. finely chopped peeled tomatoes
1/2 c. finely chopped green sweet peppers
1/2 c. finely chopped celery
1/2 c. finely chopped cucumber
1/4 c. minced onion
2 tsp. chopped parsley
1 tsp. chopped chives
1 sm. clove of garlic, pressed
2 tbsp. tarragon vinegar
2 tbsp. olive oil
1 tsp. salt
1/4 tsp. pepper
1/2 tsp. Worcestershire sauce
2 c. tomato juice

Combine all ingredients in large bowl; blend well. Cover tightly; refrigerate for at least 4 hours. Serve in chilled cups with croutons. Yield: About 6 servings.

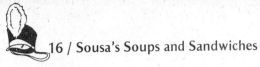

SWISS CREAM OF POTATO SOUP

4 med. potatoes, peeled
2 bacon slices, diced
1/4 c. minced onion
2 tbsp. butter
1 tbsp. chopped parsley
2 tsp. salt
1/2 tsp. nutmeg
Dash of pepper
1/4 tsp. dry mustard
1 tsp. Worcestershire sauce
3 c. milk
1/2 c. grated Swiss cheese

Cook potatoes in small amount of water in saucepan until tender; drain and mash. Saute bacon and onion over low heat, stirring, until golden brown. Add bacon mixture, butter, parsley, salt, nutmeg, pepper, mustard and Worcestershire sauce to potatoes. Stir in milk; simmer, stirring constantly, until heated through. Sprinkle with cheese; serve at once.

GULF GUMBO

1/2 c. butter
2 10-oz. packages frozen sliced okra, thawed
1/2 c. minced onion
1/2 c. minced green pepper
1/2 tsp. minced garlic
2 tbsp. flour
4 c. chicken stock
6 sprigs of parsley
1 lg. bay leaf
2 c. coarsely chopped tomatoes
1/2 tsp. thyme
2 tsp. salt
Pepper to taste
1 lb. small shrimp, shelled and deveined
1/2 lb. lump crab meat
16 oysters
2 tsp. lemon juice
2 tsp. Worcestershire sauce
1 tbsp. file powder
1/4 tsp. hot sauce
2 c. hot cooked rice

Melt 1/4 cup butter in large skillet over moderate heat. Add okra; cook, stirring constantly, until tender. Melt remaining butter in 3-quart Dutch oven over moderate heat. Add onion, green pepper and garlic; cook for about 5 minutes or until onion is transparent. Stir in flour; cook for about 3 minutes longer, stirring constantly. Pour in chicken stock; stir until mixed. Tie parsley and bay leaf together; add to onion mixture. Add okra, tomatoes, thyme, salt and pepper. Bring to a boil; reduce heat. Simmer, partially covered, for 30 minutes. Add shrimp; simmer for 5 minutes. Add crab meat and oysters; simmer for about 3 minutes or until oysters curl around edges. Remove from heat. Stir in lemon juice, Worcestershire sauce, file and hot sauce; serve over rice. Yield: 8-10 servings.

When cooking eggs, it helps prevent cracking if you wet the shells in cold water before placing them in boiling water.

FAVORITE OYSTER STEW

1/4 c. margarine
1 pt. fresh oysters
1 qt. milk
1 tsp. salt
Pepper to taste

Melt margarine in saucepan; add oysters and liquor. Cook over medium heat for about 3 minutes or until edges of oysters begin to curl. Add milk and salt; bring just to boiling point. Sprinkle each serving with pepper. Yield: 4 servings.

LOW-CALORIE VEGETABLE SOUP

1 lg. onion, chopped
4 carrots, chopped
4 stalks celery, chopped
1/2 head cabbage, chopped
1 46-oz. can tomato juice
6 bouillon cubes
1 bay leaf
Salt and pepper to taste

Combine all ingredients with 3 cups water in kettle; mix well. Bring to a boil; reduce heat. Simmer for 1 hour or until vegetables are tender; remove bay leaf.

Recipes on pages 10 and 12.

GERSHWIN'S GOULASH

2 lb. ground round steak
3 tbsp. olive or salad oil
1 1-lb. 12-oz. can tomatoes
1 qt. tomato juice
2 c. chopped onions
3 cloves of garlic, minced
Salt
2 tbsp. chili powder
1/2 tsp. ground cumin seed
1/2 tsp. ground oregano
1/2 tsp. pepper
1 bay leaf
1 15-oz. can red kidney beans, drained
1 c. chopped sweet mixed pickles
3 qt. rapidly boiling water
2 c. elbow macaroni

Cook ground steak in oil in Dutch oven until brown, stirring frequently. Add tomatoes, tomato juice, onions, garlic, 4 teaspoons salt and remaining seasonings; cover. Simmer for 1 hour; stir in kidney beans and pickles. Cook for 30 minutes longer; remove bay leaf. Add 1 tablespoon salt to boiling water. Add macaroni gradually so water continues to boil. Cook, uncovered, stirring occasionally, until tender; drain in colander. Combine with goulash; heat through. Serve in individual bowls. Yield: 10 servings.

RAGTIME RAGOUT

1 1/2 lb. beef chuck, cut into cubes
1 tbsp. shortening
1 clove of garlic, minced
1 med. onion, chopped
1/2 tsp. salt
1/8 tsp. pepper
1 can tomato soup
1 can consomme
1/4 tsp. powdered basil
1/4 tsp. powdered thyme
1/2 c. catsup
3 med. carrots
2 stalks celery
4 med. potatoes

Cook beef in shortening in Dutch oven until lightly browned. Add garlic and onion; saute until onion is transparent. Sprinkle with salt and pepper. Stir in

Recipes on pages 11, 25 and 54.

soup, consomme and 1/4 cup water; cover. Simmer for 30 minutes. Add basil, thyme and catsup. Cut carrots into 1/2-inch slices; cut celery into 1-inch diagonal slices. Pare and quarter potatoes. Arrange vegetables over beef mixture; cover. Simmer for 1 hour and 30 minutes or until beef and vegetables are tender, adding water, if needed. Yield: 4-6 servings.

LETTERMEN'S CLUB SANDWICHES

4 slices bacon
4 slices tomato
12 slices toasted bread, buttered
1/2 sm. cucumber, sliced
1/4 c. relish sandwich spread
4 slices cooked chicken
4 slices Muenster cheese

Cook bacon in skillet until crisp; drain. Place 1 tomato and bacon slice on each of 4 toast slices; add cucumber slices. Cover each sandwich with toast slice. Smooth sandwich spread over tops of toast slices; arrange chicken and cheese on relish spread. Top with remaining toast; place on cookie sheet. Bake in preheated 450-degree oven for 5 minutes or until cheese begins to melt. Press wooden picks through sides of sandwiches; cut into quarters. Garnish with olives and pickles. Yield: 4 servings.

BASSOON BARBECUED BEEF

1 3-lb. beef roast
2 tsp. pickling spice
1 lg. bottle catsup
2 green peppers, minced
1 lg. onion, minced
2 tsp. sugar
2 tsp. vinegar
1 tsp. dry mustard
1 tsp. salt

Place roast on large sheet of foil; seal. Place roast in shallow pan. Bake in preheated 350-degree oven for 2 hours. Pierce foil to let steam escape; reserve pan juices. Chill roast. Tie pickling spice in small bag; combine with catsup, green peppers, onion, 1/3 cup water, sugar, vinegar, mustard and salt. Simmer for 30 minutes, stirring frequently. Cut roast into cubes; add to catsup mixture. Add reserved pan juices; simmer until heated through. Remove spice bag. Serve beef mixture in buns.

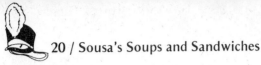

BIGGER AND BETTER BURGERS

2 lb. ground beef
2 tsp. Accent
1 1/2 tsp. salt
1/2 tsp. Tabasco sauce
Barbecue Sauce

Break up ground beef with fork; sprinkle with Accent and salt. Add Tabasco sauce and 1/2 cup water; mix lightly. Shape into 4 to 8 patties; do not mash or pound patties. Grill 4 to 5 inches from coals for 5 to 8 minutes on each side or to desired doneness. Cooking time will depend on thickness of patties and heat of charcoal. Brush patties frequently with Barbecue Sauce during grilling or just before removing from grill.

Barbecue Sauce

3 tbsp. butter or margarine
1/3 c. chopped onion
1 tsp. Accent
1/2 tsp. Tabasco sauce
1 c. catsup
1/2 c. water
1/3 c. lemon juice or vinegar
2 tbsp. Worcestershire sauce
2 tbsp. molasses
1 tbsp. prepared mustard
1/8 tsp. salt

Melt butter in saucepan; saute onion until tender but not brown. Sprinkle Accent over onion; add Tabasco sauce and remaining ingredients. Simmer for 10 minutes, stirring occasionally.

Photograph for this recipe on page 69.

SATURDAY NIGHT SLOPPY JOES

1 lb. hamburger
1/2 c. chopped onion
1/2 c. catsup
1 tbsp. prepared mustard
Salt and pepper to taste
1 can chicken gumbo soup
Hamburger buns

Cook hamburger and onion in skillet until brown. Add remaining ingredients except buns; simmer for about 30 minutes or until thick. Spread on hamburger buns. May be served over rice, if desired.

HEARTY RIPE OLIVEBURGERS

1 c. grated Cheddar cheese
2 tbsp. light cream
3/4 c. pitted California ripe olives
1/4 c. chopped green onion
1 1/2 tsp. salt
1/4 tsp. pepper
2 tsp. prepared mustard
1 1/2 lb. ground lean beef
4 hamburger rolls
Butter (opt.)
1 tbsp. oil

Combine cheese and cream. Cut 1/2 cup ripe olives into wedges. Stir into cheese mixture; set aside. Chop remaining 1/4 cup olives. Mix chopped olives, onion, salt, pepper, mustard and ground beef together. Shape into 8 patties about 1/2 inch larger in diameter than rolls. Split rolls; spread with butter. Toast lightly. Heat oil; saute patties on both sides until brown. Top patties with cheese mixture; place under broiler. Broil just long enough to melt cheese. Place 1 patty on bottom half of roll. Top with second patty; cover with top of roll. Garnish with a whole ripe olive.

Photograph for this recipe on page 14.

BUNSTEADS

1 7-oz. can tuna
1/2 lb. American cheese
3 hard-cooked eggs, chopped
2 tbsp. chopped green pepper
1 tbsp. chopped stuffed olives
2 tbsp. chopped sweet pickles
1/2 c. salad dressing or mayonnaise
6 frankfurter buns, split

Drain and flake tuna; cut cheese into small cubes. Combine tuna, cheese, eggs, green pepper, olives, pickles and salad dressing; mix well. Fill buns with tuna mixture; wrap individually in foil. Place on baking sheet. Bake in preheated 250-degree oven for about 30 minutes or until cheese melts. Yield: 6 servings.

GO-FOR-TWO TUNA SANDWICHES

1 loaf thin-sliced bread
1 can tuna
1 med. apple, chopped fine
1 hard-boiled egg, diced
1 sm. onion, chopped fine
2 sweet pickles, minced
1/2 c. finely chopped pecans
1/2 c. diced celery
Mayonnaise

Trim crusts from bread. Drain tuna; flake. Combine tuna with remaining ingredients, adding enough mayonnaise to moisten; spread between bread slices.

ALL-AMERICAN PIMENTO CHEESE SPREAD

1 lg. can evaporated milk
1 lb. American cheese, grated
2 tbsp. vinegar
1/2 tsp. dry mustard
1 7-oz. can pimentos, drained and chopped
1 tsp. salt
Dash of cayenne pepper

Scald milk in double boiler. Add remaining ingredients; cook, stirring, until cheese melts. Remove from heat; cool. Store in covered jars. Use spread for sandwiches, on crackers or for stuffing celery.

FROSTED RIBBON LOAF

1 unsliced sandwich loaf
Softened butter
Ham Filling
Egg Filling
Crab Filling
4 3-oz. packages cream cheese, softened
1/3 c. milk
Minced parsley

Remove crust from bread; cut lengthwise into 4 equal slices. Butter tops of 3 slices; spread 1 buttered slice with Ham Filling, 1 with Egg Filling and 1 with Crab Filling. Stack slices; place unbuttered slice on top. Wrap in foil; chill thoroughly. Combine cream cheese and milk in mixing bowl; beat until fluffy. Place loaf on serving plate; frost sides and top with cheese mixture. Sprinkle generously with parsley. Cut into slices to serve. Yield: 10 servings.

Ham Filling

1 c. ground cooked ham
1/3 c. finely chopped celery
2 tbsp. drained pickle relish
1/2 tsp. prepared horseradish
1/4 c. mayonnaise

Combine all ingredients; mix well.

Egg Filling

4 hard-cooked eggs, chopped
1/3 c. chopped stuffed green olives
2 tbsp. chopped green onion
2 tsp. prepared mustard
1/4 c. mayonnaise

Combine all ingredients; mix well.

Crab Filling

1 can crab meat, drained
1 tbsp. lemon juice
1/4 c. mayonnaise

Remove any cartilage from crab meat. Combine all ingredients; mix well.

Swinging Salads & Salad Dressings

Salads are a wonderful source of nutrition and economy — but, best of all, salads are fun! For all those teenagers and adults who are watching their weight as well as their health, salads offer some of the most interesting taste varieties for a relatively small number of calories.

Of course, almost any favorite raw vegetable can take its place in a salad. But, meats, fish, eggs and even various pastas can also be added to make a well-rounded and delicious meal of a salad. Then, there are hot salads, cool congealed salads and refreshing fruit salads. In fact, there is probably an imaginative salad for every day of the year.

To add even more spice to this great variety, there are so many delicious salad dressings! These can be creamy, tangy, sweet, exotic or plain — and some are low-calorie, too.

The band members think the *Fresh Fruit Medley* topped with *Poppy Seed Dressing* is a heavenly delight. The cheerleaders like *Tip-Off Tuna Salad In Tomatoes*, especially when it is topped with *Never-Fail Blender Mayonnaise*. But, try the others, too — you just can't miss!

SPICED WALNUT FRUIT SALAD

2 tsp. butter
2/3 c. California walnut halves and pieces
1 tbsp. sugar
1/2 tsp. cinnamon
1 lg. red apple
4 c. torn lettuce
1/2 c. halved fresh cranberries
1 c. seeded red grapes
1 c. mayonnaise
2 tbsp. orange juice
1/4 tsp. grated orange peel

Melt butter in skillet. Add walnuts; sprinkle with sugar and cinnamon. Cook over moderate heat for about 5 minutes or until walnuts are lightly toasted. Let cool. Core apples; cut in small wedges. Place lettuce in chilled salad bowl. Arrange walnuts and fruits on top. Combine mayonnaise, orange juice and orange peel; serve over salad.

Photograph for this recipe on page 22.

APPLE-PECAN FROST

1 pkg. unflavored gelatin
3/4 c. apple or pineapple juice
3 c. applesauce
1/4 tsp. salt
2 tbsp. lemon juice
1 tsp. grated lemon rind
3/4 c. sugar
1/2 c. chopped pecans
1/2 c. heavy cream, whipped

Soften gelatin in 1/4 cup apple juice; dissolve in remaining 1/2 cup boiling apple juice. Combine applesauce, salt, lemon juice, lemon rind and sugar; stir into gelatin. Pour into large freezer tray; freeze until frozen 1 inch from edge of tray. Scrape frozen mixture into bowl; beat until light and fluffy. Fold in pecans and whipped cream. Place in freezer tray; freeze until firm. Remove from freezer 10 minutes before serving. Yield: 9-12 servings.

CHERRY SPARKLE CELEBRATION

1 1-lb. 4-oz. can crushed pineapple
1 1-lb. 4-oz. can Bing cherries, drained

2 pkg. black cherry gelatin
2 6 1/2-oz. bottles Coca-Cola

Drain pineapple; reserve syrup. Add enough water to pineapple syrup to measure 2 cups liquid. Pour liquid into saucepan; bring to a boil. Stir in gelatin until dissolved. Add Coca-Cola. Chill gelatin until partially congealed; fold in fruits. Turn into mold; chill until firm. Yield: 20 servings.

FRESH CRANBERRY SALAD

2 c. fresh cranberries
2 c. sugar
1 unpeeled apple
1 unpeeled orange
2 pkg. lemon gelatin
1 c. chopped nuts

Grind cranberries coarsely; cover with sugar. Grind apple and orange. Dissolve gelatin in 1 cup boiling water. Combine cranberries, apple, orange, gelatin and nuts; pour into mold. Chill until firm. Yield: 6-8 servings.

FRESH FRUIT MEDLEY

6 ripe peaches, peeled and diced
6 lg. plums, peeled and diced
1 c. halved cherries
1/2 c. sliced cantaloupe
1 slice watermelon, cubed
1 orange, peeled and diced
1 1/2 c. raspberries

Mix all ingredients together; chill until ready to serve. May top each serving with sour cream, if desired.

ORANGE SHERBET SALAD

1 pkg. orange gelatin
1 pt. orange sherbet, slightly thawed
1 1/2 c. mandarin orange slices, drained

Prepare gelatin according to package directions; chill until partially congealed. Beat until light and fluffy; stir in sherbet and orange slices. Pour into mold; chill until firm. Yield: 8 servings.

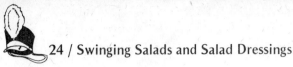

LIME AND GRAPEFRUIT MOLD

2 3-oz. packages lime gelatin
3/4 c. grapefruit juice
1 8-oz. package cream cheese, softened
1 c. ginger ale
1 c. halved grapefruit sections
1 c. diced apples
1/4 c. chopped walnuts

Dissolve 1 package lime gelatin in 1 cup boiling water; add grapefruit juice. Stir slowly into cream cheese, mixing until well blended. Pour into 1 1/2-quart mold. Chill until firm. Dissolve remaining package lime gelatin in 1 cup boiling water; add ginger ale. Chill until thickened. Fold in fruits and walnuts; pour over cheese layer. Chill until firm. Unmold onto lettuce. Yield: 6-8 servings.

TURKEY-HAM IMPERIAL

2 tbsp. unflavored gelatin
1/2 c. chicken bouillon
3/4 c. mayonnaise
3/4 tbsp. lemon juice
1 1/2 c. diced cooked turkey
3/4 c. diced smoked ham
3/4 c. minced celery
2 tbsp. chopped green pepper
1/2 c. chopped almonds
3/4 c. whipped cream
Salt and pepper to taste

Soften gelatin in bouillon. Place over boiling water; stir until dissolved. Combine gelatin mixture, mayonnaise, lemon juice, turkey, ham, celery, green pepper, almonds, whipped cream and seasonings. Pour into oiled mold. Chill for 6 hours or until set. Unmold on serving tray. Garnish with cherry tomatoes and cucumber slices.

ORIGINAL SHRIMP LOUIS

1 c. mayonnaise
1 tbsp. tarragon vinegar
3 tbsp. chili sauce
1 tsp. Worcestershire sauce
2 tbsp. chopped pimento
1 clove of garlic, crushed
1 tsp. salt
1 tsp. powdered sugar

1 tsp. paprika
1/4 tsp. mustard
Lettuce leaves
Cooked shrimp

Combine mayonnaise, vinegar, chili sauce and Worcestershire sauce. Add pimento, garlic, salt, sugar, paprika and mustard; mix well. Cover; chill until ready to serve. Arrange lettuce leaves on plate; place desired number of shrimp in center. Pour sauce over shrimp. Garnish with tomato quarters and hard-boiled egg wedges, if desired.

TIP-OFF TUNA SALAD IN TOMATOES

6 tomatoes
Lettuce
1 7-oz. can tuna, drained
3 hard-cooked eggs, chopped
5 radishes, minced
1/4 c. minced celery
1/4 c. minced green pepper
1/2 tsp. garlic salt
1 tsp. pepper
Salad dressing

Cut tomatoes into wedges almost to bottom; spread wedges. Arrange tomatoes on 6 lettuce-lined plates. Combine remaining ingredients, using enough salad dressing to moisten to desired consistency. Pile salad lightly into tomato cups.

VEGETABLES VINAIGRETTE

2 c. cauliflowerets
2 10-oz. packages frozen artichoke hearts
3 tsp. Accent
2 c. shredded carrots
2 c. halved cherry tomatoes or tomato wedges
2 cucumbers, peeled and cut in wedges
Vinaigrette Dressing
2 qt. broken salad greens

Place cauliflowerets and artichoke hearts in separate saucepans. Cover with cold water; add 1 teaspoon

To keep egg yolks from crumbling when slicing hard-cooked eggs, wet the knife before each cut.

Accent to each saucepan. Bring to a boil over high heat. Remove from heat; drain well. Place cauliflowerets, artichoke hearts, carrots, tomatoes and cucumber wedges in separate bowls; add about 1/3 cup Vinaigrette Dressing to each bowl. Let vegetables marinate in refrigerator for 2 hours or longer, stirring occasionally. Place salad greens in bowl; sprinkle with remaining 1 teaspoon Accent. Drain vegetables; reserve marinade. Arrange vegetables on salad greens in wedge pattern; serve reserved marinade as dressing.

Vinaigrette Dressing

2/3 c. vinegar
1 1/2 tsp. salt
1 tsp. sugar
1/4 tsp. Tabasco sauce
2 tsp. dillweed
1 tsp. instant minced onion
1 1/3 c. salad oil

Pour vinegar into quart jar. Add salt, sugar, Tabasco sauce, dillweed and onion; shake well. Add salad oil; shake until thoroughly mixed.

Photograph for this recipe on page 69.

DAD'S FAVORITE SALAD

1 lg. head romaine
1   15 1/4-oz. can kidney beans, drained
1 lg. cucumber, pared and cubed
1 sm. carrot, pared and shredded
1   8-oz. bottle chunky blue cheese dressing
2 tbsp. dry sherry
1/4 tsp. Tabasco sauce

Tear romaine into bite-sized pieces, removing coarse ribs. Combine romaine, kidney beans, cucumber and carrot in large bowl. Mix blue cheese dressing, sherry and Tabasco sauce together; serve with salad. Yield: 6 to 8 servings.

Photograph for this recipe on page 36.

CONFETTI COLESLAW

4 c. shredded cabbage
1/2 c. shredded carrot
1 tsp. salt
1 tsp. sugar
1/2 c. mayonnaise
1 tbsp. vinegar
1 tbsp. milk
1 sm. red apple, chopped

Sprinkle cabbage and carrot with salt and sugar. Combine mayonnaise, vinegar and milk. Add to cabbage mixture; mix well. Chill thoroughly. Toss in apple just before serving. Yield: 8 servings.

Photograph for this recipe on page 18.

MACARONI SUPPER SALAD

1 c. cooked seashell macaroni
2 1/2 c. chopped cooked ham
6 hard-boiled eggs, chopped
1/4 c. minced sweet pickles
5 green onions, thinly sliced
1/4 c. minced green pepper
1 c. mayonnaise
Salt and pepper to taste
Paprika to taste

Combine all ingredients in large bowl; mix well. Chill for several hours before serving. Yield: 8-10 servings.

PIQUANT STUFFED EGGS

6 hard-boiled eggs
1 tbsp. ground toasted almonds
3 tbsp. mayonnaise
4 tsp. tomato juice
1 1/2 tbsp. freshly grated Parmesan cheese
1/8 tsp. white pepper
1/4 tsp. salt

Cut eggs into halves. Remove yolks; place yolks in small mixing bowl. Mash with fork until fine. Add remaining ingredients; mix until smooth. Stuff yolk mixture into egg whites.

DELICIOUS DIET DRESSING

2 c. cottage cheese
1 c. buttermilk
1 tbsp. red wine vinegar
2 tbsp. chopped parsley
3/4 tsp. seasoned salt

Place cottage cheese in blender container; blend until smooth and creamy. Add buttermilk, vinegar, parsley and seasoned salt; blend until combined. Cover; store in refrigerator. Will keep for about 2 weeks.

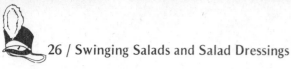

ZESTY FRENCH DRESSING

1 med. onion, grated
1 clove of garlic, pressed (opt.)
1/2 c. sugar
1/3 c. catsup
1 tsp. salt
1 tsp. Worcestershire sauce
1 c. Mazola oil
1/4 c. vinegar

Combine onion, garlic, sugar, catsup, salt, Worcestershire sauce and oil. Add vinegar; beat until thick. Keep refrigerated.

ELEGANT CHEESE MOLD

1 carton cream-style cottage cheese
2   3-oz. packages cream cheese
1 env. unflavored gelatin
1/4 tsp. salt
1 c. seedless green grapes
1/2 c. broken pecans

2 tbsp. chopped chives
1 c. heavy cream, whipped

Bring cheeses to room temperature; blend thoroughly. Soften gelatin in 1/4 cup cold water; dissolve over boiling water. Add salt; stir into cheese mixture. Add grapes, pecans and chives; fold in whipped cream. Spoon into individual molds or one 1-quart mold. Chill for 4 to 6 hours.

CLASSIC BOILED DRESSING

1/4 c. sugar
1 tsp. dry mustard
1 tsp. salt
2 tbsp. cornstarch
2 tbsp. vinegar
2 tbsp. lemon juice
2 tbsp. butter
2 egg yolks, beaten

Combine sugar, mustard, salt and cornstarch in saucepan; stir in vinegar, lemon juice, 1 1/2 cups water and butter. Cook over low heat until thickened, stirring frequently. Add a small amount of hot mixture to egg yolks gradually, stirring constantly. Stir egg yolk mixture into lemon juice mixture gradually; cook for 1 minute longer. Remove from heat; cool. Place in jar; cover. Keep refrigerated.

NEVER-FAIL BLENDER MAYONNAISE

1 c. salad oil
2 tbsp. lemon juice
1 egg
1/2 tsp. salt
1/8 tsp. paprika
1/4 tsp. dry mustard
Dash of cayenne pepper

Pour 1/4 cup of the oil into electric blender container; add lemon juice, egg and seasonings. Cover; blend for 5 seconds. Remove cover while blender is running; add remaining oil in a thin steady stream. Turn off blender immediately after adding oil. Yield: 1 1/2 cups.

POPPY SEED DRESSING

1 egg
1/4 c. sugar
1/4 c. lemon juice
1 tbsp. poppy seed
1 tsp. dry mustard
1 tsp. grated onion
1/2 tsp. paprika
1/2 tsp. salt
1 1/2 c. salad oil
1/4 c. honey

Place egg, sugar, lemon juice, poppy seed, mustard, onion, paprika and salt in blender container. Blend at high speed, adding oil gradually. Add honey; blend at medium speed until well mixed. Yield: 2 cups.

ROYAL ROQUEFORT DRESSING

1/2 lb. Roquefort cheese
3 hard-cooked eggs
1 tsp. onion, minced
1 clove of garlic, minced (opt.)
1 tsp. sugar
1/4 c. vinegar
1 tsp. Worcestershire sauce
2 c. salad oil

Combine cheese, egg yolks, onion and garlic to make a paste, using fork. Add sugar, vinegar and Worcestershire sauce; mix well. Stir in chopped egg whites and salad oil; mix thoroughly.

ITALIAN DRESSING

1/2 c. (packed) brown sugar
1/2 c. vinegar
1/2 c. catsup
1/2 c. salad oil
1 sm. onion, minced
1 clove of garlic, minced
Pinch of dry mustard
Salt and pepper to taste

Combine all ingredients; blend thoroughly.

CREAMY RUSSIAN DRESSING

1/2 c. tomato sauce
6 tbsp. white vinegar
3/4 c. salad oil
1 sm. clove of garlic, chopped
1/2 sm. onion, chopped
1/2 c. sugar
1 tbsp. dry mustard
1 tbsp. salt
1 tbsp. Worcestershire sauce
1/2 tsp. paprika
2 drops of Tabasco sauce

Place all ingredients in blender container; process until well blended. Dressing may be prepared by mincing garlic and onion; beat with remaining ingredients until well blended. Yield: 2 cups.

THOUSAND ISLAND DRESSING SUPREME

4 egg yolks
1/2 tsp. salt
1/2 tsp. dry mustard
1/2 tsp. sugar
3 tbsp. vinegar
1 qt. Wesson oil
1/2 c. chopped pickles
1 onion, finely chopped
1 c. catsup
4 hard-boiled eggs, chopped

Beat egg yolks, salt, mustard, sugar and vinegar together at high speed of electric mixer; add oil slowly. Beat at low speed for 15 minutes. Stir in remaining ingredients. Dressing keeps well. Yield: 2 quarts.

Marching Meats

Lineup . . . Sound-Off . . . March . . . *Extra Point Pork Dinner, Veal Variation, Meat Roll Masterpiece* and many other delicious meat dishes are heading your way. Meat is just as important to a well-balanced meal as a band and cheerleaders are to a spirited ball game. Even though wise mothers know this, preparing a different meat dish everyday often becomes quite a problem.

Whether your family prefers beef, ground beef, pork, veal or lamb, the variety of recipes here is sure to enliven your weekly menu. Make-ahead casseroles for those too-busy-to-cook days, roasts to feed family and guests, and after-the-game pick-me-ups are just a few of the delightful taste treats that you can prepare. To be sure, keeping in step with your family's likes and dislikes can be quite difficult. But, nothing can bring hungry boys and girls running faster than the aroma of their favorite meat roasting in the oven or sizzling on the grill.

Now you can have as much fun concocting new dishes in the kitchen as your family has taste-testing them at the dinner table. By trying any of these Marching Meats recipes, you can make the main course at your next meal one to remember.

BEEF TIPS NAPOLI

3 lb. boneless beef chuck
1 tsp. salt
1/4 tsp. pepper
2 tbsp. salad oil
2 6-oz. cans tomato paste
2 tbsp. lemon juice
1/2 tsp. sugar
1 tsp. marjoram or oregano
1 sm. carrot, thinly sliced
1 clove of garlic, minced
1 lb. seashell macaroni
1/4 c. grated Parmesan cheese
2 tbsp. chopped parsley

Cut beef into 2-inch cubes; sprinkle with salt and pepper. Brown in oil in large skillet. Mix tomato paste with 1 1/2 cups water, lemon juice, sugar, marjoram, carrot and garlic; pour over beef. Cover. Simmer for 1 hour and 30 minutes to 2 hours or until beef is tender, adding water and salt, if needed. Cook macaroni according to package directions; drain well. Mix with cheese and parsley. Serve beef mixture over macaroni mixture. Yield: 6 servings.

BEEF STROGANOFF

1 1-lb. sirloin or round steak
2 tbsp. flour
1/3 tsp. salt
1/4 tsp. pepper
1/2 c. chopped onions
1 clove of garlic, minced
1/4 c. butter or oil
1 can beef consomme
1 lb. mushrooms, sliced
1/2 bottle chili sauce
1 c. sour cream

Trim beef; cut in thin slices. Combine flour, salt and pepper in bag. Add beef slices; shake until well floured. Brown onions and garlic lightly in butter in large skillet; remove from skillet. Saute beef slices until browned. Cover with water; simmer for 15 minutes. Add consomme, mushrooms, onion mixture and chili sauce. Cover; cook for 30 minutes longer. Remove cover; cook until beef is tender. Add sour cream just before serving. Do not boil after adding sour cream. Can be made ahead and frozen.

EASY COMPANY ROAST BEEF

1 6-lb. fresh beef brisket
Salt and pepper to taste
Thyme to taste
1 onion, minced
4 stalks celery, minced
2 or 3 carrots, minced

Place brisket in roaster; sprinkle with salt, pepper and thyme. Combine vegetables; spread over top of brisket. Cover. Bake in preheated 250-degree oven for 6 hours or until tender. Slice brisket cross grain. Serve with pan juices. May add potatoes during last hour of cooking, if desired.

POT ROAST WITH TOMATO GRAVY

1 4 to 5-lb. beef blade pot roast
1 clove of garlic (opt.)
1/2 tsp. thyme
1/2 c. vinegar
Salt and pepper to taste
1 No. 303 can tomatoes
1/4 c. flour
Cooked noodles

Brown roast in 1/4 cup fat in Dutch oven. Add garlic, thyme, vinegar, salt, pepper and 1/3 cup water. Cover; cook over low heat for 2 hours. Add tomatoes; simmer for about 1 hour longer or until roast is tender. Remove roast to hot platter. Remove garlic and discard. Mix flour with 1/4 cup water; stir into tomato mixture. Cook until thick, stirring constantly; pour over noodles. Serve with roast.

STEAK WITH GARLIC SAUCE

3 tbsp. butter
1 tsp. garlic powder
3 tbsp. Worcestershire sauce
1/2 c. steak sauce
1 2 1/2-lb. sirloin steak

Melt butter in saucepan over low heat. Add garlic powder, Worcestershire sauce and steak sauce; stir until mixed. Bring to boiling point; remove from heat. Place steak on broiler pan; brush with steak sauce mixture. Broil 3 inches from source of heat for 5 minutes. Turn steak; brush with steak sauce mixture. Broil for 5 minutes longer or to desired doneness. Yield: 4 servings.

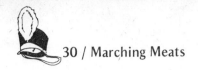

A large roast can be carved more easily after it stands for about thirty minutes.

CARPETBAG STEAK

12 to 18 oysters
1 lb. mushrooms, chopped
3/4 c. butter
1 c. bread crumbs
1 tbsp. parsley flakes
Grated rind of 1/2 lemon
Salt and paprika to taste
1 egg, beaten
1 2-in. thick boned sirloin steak with pocket

Place oysters and mushrooms in heated butter; cook for 5 minutes. Transfer to bowl; stir in bread crumbs, parsley, lemon rind, salt and paprika. Add egg; mix well. Press into pocket in steak; sew or skewer edges together. Place in baking pan. Bake in preheated 325-degree oven for 1 hour or until done. Cut steak crosswise into 6 servings.

FANCY FLANK STEAK

1/4 c. soy sauce
3 tbsp. honey
2 tbsp. vinegar
1 1/2 tsp. garlic powder
1 1/2 tsp. ginger
3/4 c. salad oil
1 green onion, minced
1 1 1/2-lb. flank steak

Combine soy sauce, honey and vinegar; blend in garlic powder and ginger. Stir in oil and green onion for marinade. Place steak in shallow pan; cover with marinade. Let stand for at least 4 hours. Place steak on grill over hot coals. Broil for 5 minutes on each side for medium rare, basting occasionally with marinade. Yield: 4 servings.

PEPPERED TENDERLOIN

2 lb. beef tenderloin or sirloin
4 tbsp. margarine or butter
2 tbsp. olive oil

1 tsp. salt
1/2 tsp. coarsely ground pepper
Dash of ground sage
Dash of ground cumin
1 lb. mushrooms, quartered
2 cloves of garlic, minced
1 med. onion, cut in wedges
2 med. green peppers, cubed
2 tomatoes, cut in wedges
1/2 c. soy sauce
2 tbsp. cider vinegar
2 tbsp. tomato paste

Slice beef in 1/4-inch wide strips. Saute several strips at a time in 2 tablespoons margarine and 1 tablespoon olive oil in large frying pan. Place in 4-quart baking dish. Sprinkle with salt, pepper, sage and cumin; toss lightly to mix. Saute mushrooms in remaining 2 tablespoons margarine and 1 tablespoon olive oil in same pan for 2 minutes; add to beef. Stir garlic, onion and green peppers into pan drippings; saute for 2 minutes. Add to beef with tomatoes. Combine soy sauce, vinegar and tomato paste in pan; bring to a boil, stirring constantly. Pour over beef; toss lightly to mix. Bake, covered, in preheated 350-degree oven for 30 minutes or until heated through. Yield: 6 servings.

ITALIAN LONDON BROIL

2 2-lb. flank steaks
1 8-oz. bottle real Italian dressing
1/2 c. dry sherry
1/4 c. red wine vinegar
1/2 tsp. Tabasco sauce

Trim excess fat and membrane from steaks. Score lightly or pierce steaks. Place in shallow dish. Combine dressing, sherry, vinegar and Tabasco sauce; pour over steaks. Let marinate at room temperature for 2 hours, turning steaks every 30 minutes. Broil or grill steaks 2 inches from source of heat for 5 minutes on each side. Must be very rare to be tender. Cut in thin slices diagonally against the grain to serve. Yield: 6 to 8 servings.

Photograph for this recipe on page 36.

DRIED BEEF SUPREME

1 sm. jar dried beef
2 tbsp. butter or margarine

1 med. green pepper, chopped
1 can mushroom soup
1 sm. can mushroom pieces
1/2 soup can milk

Cut dried beef into small pieces. Melt butter in saucepan; saute dried beef and green pepper lightly. Add soup and mushroom pieces; stir in milk. Heat through. May be served over toast or hot grits. Yield: 4 servings.

OLD-FASHIONED LIVER AND ONIONS

1 1/2 lb. sliced calf liver
Seasoned flour
6 med. onions, thinly sliced
4 slices crisp bacon, crumbled

Dredge liver with seasoned flour; saute in hot fat until slightly brown. Place in greased baking dish. Cover with onions. Season with salt and pepper; sprinkle with bacon. Add 1/2 cup hot water; cover. Bake in preheated 350-degree oven for 30 minutes, adding more water if needed. Remove cover; bake 10 minutes longer. Yield: 2-4 servings.

CONFETTI CASSEROLE

1 1/2 lb. ground beef chuck
1/2 c. chopped onion
3/4 c. milk
1 8-oz. package cream cheese
2 12-oz. cans whole kernel corn with red and green peppers
1/2 c. diced canned pimento
1 can cream of mushroom soup
1 1/2 tsp. salt
1/4 tsp. pepper
1 8-oz. package med. noodles, cooked
1/4 c. shredded Parmesan cheese

Brown beef in large skillet. Add onion; saute until tender. Drain off excess fat. Stir in milk. Add cream cheese; stir until smooth. Mix in corn, pimento, soup, salt, pepper and noodles; place in large casserole. Sprinkle top with cheese. Bake in preheated 350-degree oven for about 45 minutes or until hot and bubbly. Place under broiler to brown, if desired. May be frozen. Yield: 8 servings.

FIFTH QUARTER CASSEROLE

1 lb. ground beef
1 c. chopped onions
1 c. bean sprouts
1 can cream of mushroom soup
1 can cream of chicken soup
1 1/2 c. water
1 1/2 tbsp. soy sauce
1/2 c. rice
1 c. Chinese noodles

Cook and stir ground beef until browned. Add onions; cook until tender. Drain off fat. Add remaining ingredients except noodles; mix well. Place in casserole; cover. Bake in preheated 350-degree oven for 30 minutes. Uncover; bake for 30 minutes longer. Sprinkle noodles on top; bake for about 15 minutes or until noodles are heated through and browned. Yield: 8-10 servings.

LASAGNA TREAT

2 lb. ground beef
1/2 c. chopped onion
3 tsp. oregano
3 tsp. Italian seasoning
2 tsp. garlic salt
2 tsp. salt
1 tsp. pepper
3/4 c. minced parsley
2 6-oz. cans tomato paste
4 tomato paste cans water
1 ball mozzarella cheese
2 c. small curd cottage cheese
1 box lasagna noodles

Combine ground beef, onion, seasonings and 1/2 cup parsley in skillet; cook until ground beef is brown, stirring frequently. Add tomato paste and water; simmer for 3 to 4 hours or until thickened, stirring occasionally. Shred cheese; combine with cottage cheese and remaining 1/4 cup parsley. Cook noodles according to package directions; rinse well. Spoon layer of tomato sauce in 10 or 12-inch square baking dish; add thin layer of cheese mixture. Top with layer of noodles. Continue layers, ending with cheese mixture. Bake in preheated 350-degree oven for 45 minutes to 1 hour or until heated through. Lasagna may be prepared in 2 baking dishes; one may be frozen for later use.

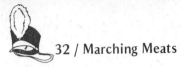

CRANBERRY FOOTBALL LOAF

2 lb. ground lean chuck
3 eggs
1 pkg. stuffing mix
1 c. Ocean Spray cranberry-orange relish
1 onion, chopped
4 strips bacon, fried crisp and crumbled
1 c. tomato juice
4 c. seasoned mashed potatoes
Pimento strips

Combine all ingredients except potatoes and pimento strips; shape mixture into football-shaped loaf. Place on greased, foil-lined shallow baking pan. Bake in preheated 350-degree oven for 1 hour or until juices run clear when loaf is pierced. Place loaf on platter; spoon mashed potatoes around loaf. Garnish top with strips of pimento to resemble laces on top of a football. Sprinkle potatoes with chopped parsley, if desired. Yield: 10-12 servings.

Photograph for this recipe on page 28.

MAIN ATTRACTION MEATBALLS

1 1/2 lb. ground beef
1 onion, minced
2 tsp. salt
1/4 tsp. pepper
1 egg
3 tbsp. bread crumbs
1/4 c. shortening
1 lb. mushrooms, sliced
Butter
2 egg yolks
2 tbsp. lemon juice

Combine beef, onion, salt, pepper, 3 tablespoons water, egg and bread crumbs; form into small meatballs. Fry in shortening until well browned. Cook mushrooms in small amount of butter in frypan until brown. Beat egg yolks with lemon juice; stir slowly into mushrooms. Add mushroom mixture to meatballs; cook for 15 minutes longer, stirring frequently.

MEAT ROLL MASTERPIECE

2 eggs, beaten
2 slices bread, crumbled
1/2 c. tomato juice
2 tbsp. chopped parsley
1 clove of garlic, minced
1/2 tsp. oregano leaves
1 tsp. salt
1/4 tsp. pepper
2 lb. ground beef round
8 slices boiled ham or luncheon meat
6 oz. mozzarella cheese, shredded
3 slices mozzarella cheese, halved diagonally

Combine eggs, bread crumbs, tomato juice, parsley, garlic, oregano and seasonings. Add beef; mix well. Pat beef mixture to 14 x 12-inch rectangle; cover with ham, leaving 1 1/2-inch margin on all sides. Sprinkle shredded cheese over ham. Roll up as for jelly roll; seal edges. Place in baking pan, seam side down. Bake in preheated 350-degree oven for 1 hour and 15 minutes or to desired doneness. Top with cheese slices; bake until cheese is melted. Yield: 8 servings.

EASY ENCHILADA PIE

1 lb. ground beef
1 c. chopped onions
1 clove of garlic, minced
2 tbsp. butter
1 tsp. salt
1/4 tsp. pepper
1 tbsp. chili powder
1 4 1/2-oz. can chopped black olives
1 8-oz. can tomato sauce
6 corn tortillas, buttered
2 c. grated Cheddar cheese
2/3 c. water

Saute ground beef, onions and garlic in butter until lightly browned; add seasonings, olives and tomato sauce. Place layers of tortillas, beef sauce and cheese in round 2-quart casserole, ending with cheese. Pour water, at edge, into casserole; cover. Bake in preheated 400-degree oven for 30 minutes or until done. Cut into wedges to serve. Yield: 4-6 servings.

CHEESE CRUST BEEF PIE

1 1/2 lb. ground beef
2 tbsp. diced green pepper
1 3/4 tsp. salt
1/8 tsp. garlic powder
1/4 tsp. pepper

1 1/4 c. flour
3 c. tomato juice
2/3 c. diced celery
2 tsp. Worcestershire sauce
1/3 c. shortening
1/3 c. grated sharp cheese

Brown ground beef and green pepper lightly in 10-inch skillet; drain off excess fat. Add 1 1/2 teaspoons salt, garlic powder and pepper. Mix in 1/4 cup flour; add tomato juice, stirring constantly. Add celery and Worcestershire sauce; simmer for 15 minutes. Pour into 9-inch square baking dish. Cut shortening into remaining 1 cup flour and 1/4 teaspoon salt. Add cheese; mix well. Add 1/4 cup water, stirring with fork until pastry holds together. Roll out on floured waxed paper. Place crust over top of beef mixture; seal edges. Cut several vents in center. Bake in preheated 425-degree oven for 30 minutes or until bubbly.

SAUSAGE PIZZA

1 1/2 c. milk, scalded
1/2 c. lard
2 tsp. salt
1 pkg. or 1 cake yeast
1/2 c. lukewarm water
6 c. sifted flour
2 lb. fresh pork sausage
3 c. tomato sauce
2 tbsp. grated Parmesan cheese
1 tbsp. leaf oregano
1 tbsp. sugar
2 c. grated mozzarella cheese

Combine milk, lard and salt in large bowl. Let cool to lukewarm. Dissolve yeast in water; let stand for 10 minutes. Add to milk mixture. Add 5 cups flour; mix thoroughly. Turn out dough on a floured board; knead for about 5 minutes, adding remaining 1 cup flour to form a soft dough, if needed. Place on greased pizza pan. Cover; let rise in a warm place for about 1 hour or until doubled in bulk. Divide dough in half. Roll each half into 14-inch circle; place each on greased 14-inch pizza pan, pressing out to edge of pan. Saute sausage in large frypan until light brown, breaking sausage into small pieces. Drain on paper toweling. Combine tomato sauce, Parmesan cheese, oregano and sugar; spread half the mixture over each dough-lined pizza pan. Sprinkle half of the sausage and half the mozzarella cheese over tomato sauce mixture. Bake in preheated 450-degree oven for 12 to 15 minutes or until done.

Photograph for this recipe on the cover.

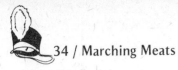

LAMB CURRY

1 1/2 lb. boneless lamb shoulder
6 tbsp. butter
2 lg. onions, thinly sliced
2 cloves of garlic, crushed
1 c. finely chopped celery
2 lg. cooking apples, pared and sliced
3 lg. tomatoes, cut in wedges
1/4 tsp. ginger
1 1/2 tbsp. curry powder
1 tbsp. sugar
1 1/2 tsp. salt
1/4 tsp. pepper
1/4 c. cornstarch
3 c. cooked rice

Cut lamb into 1-inch cubes. Melt 2 tablespoons butter in skillet; saute lamb, turning to brown well on all sides. Add 2 cups water; reduce heat. Simmer, covered, for 1 hour or until lamb is tender. Remove lamb from skillet; pour off and reserve pan juices. Melt remaining 4 tablespoons butter in skillet. Stir in onions, garlic and celery. Cook, stirring frequently, until onions are lightly browned. Add apples, tomatoes, ginger, curry powder, sugar, salt and pepper; blend well. Stir in lamb. Add enough water to reserved pan juices to measure 3 cups liquid. Add to lamb mixture. Combine cornstarch with small amount of water. Stir cornstarch mixture into lamb mixture; blend thoroughly. Simmer, covered, for 5 minutes or until heated through, stirring as necessary. Serve with rice. Yield: 6-8 servings.

LAMB CHOPS WITH SPINACH DRESSING

1 med. onion, minced
6 lamb shoulder chops
2 tsp. salt
4 1/2 c. chopped fresh spinach
4 1/2 c. fine soft bread crumbs
2 eggs
Celery salt to taste

Saute onion in 1 tablespoon fat in skillet until soft. Remove from skillet; set aside. Season chops with 1/2 teaspoon salt; brown in skillet on both sides over low heat. Combine spinach, bread crumbs, onion, eggs, remaining 1 1/2 teaspoons salt and celery salt; blend well. Place spinach dressing in shallow baking dish; place lamb chops on top. Bake, covered, in preheated 350-degree oven for 1 hour or until the chops are tender.

COACH'S SPECIAL

1/2 c. water
2 tbsp. vinegar
1 tbsp. Worcestershire sauce
1/4 c. lemon juice
1 tsp. dry mustard
Dash of Tabasco sauce
1/4 tsp. paprika
1 clove of garlic, minced
1 onion, grated
1 tbsp. salad oil
1/3 c. catsup
1/2 tsp. salt
1 leg of lamb, boned and rolled

Combine all ingredients except lamb in saucepan; bring to a boil, stirring to mix well. Place lamb in large bowl; pour marinade over lamb. Cover; let stand in refrigerator for 2 to 3 days, turning occasionally. Remove lamb; reserve marinade. Center lamb on barbecue spit. Insert meat thermometer in thickest part of leg; do not let tip of thermometer touch metal spit. Cook over hot coals until thermometer registers done, basting frequently with reserved marinade.

ROCKY MOUNTAIN LAMB

1 12-oz. bottle hot catsup
1/2 c. orange juice
1/4 c. chopped parsley
1/4 tsp. celery seed
1/4 tsp. rosemary leaves
3 lb. lamb riblets

Combine catsup, orange juice, parsley, celery seed and rosemary leaves. Cut riblets into serving pieces; place in shallow oblong dish. Pour sauce over riblets; let marinate in refrigerator overnight. Drain riblets; reserve marinade. Brown riblets well in hot fat in skillet. Arrange riblets in baking dish; add reserved marinade. Cover baking dish. Bake in preheated 375-degree oven for 35 to 40 minutes or until tender. Yield: 4 servings.

Recipe on page 38.

HAM-STUFFED PORK CHOPS

3 c. fresh bread crumbs
1 c. chopped cooked ham
1/8 tsp. pepper
1/4 tsp. nutmeg
1 egg, beaten
1 can beef broth
6 pork chops, 1 1/2 in. thick
1 tsp. salt
1/4 tsp. sage
1/4 tsp. thyme
Salad oil
Cornstarch

Combine bread crumbs, ham, pepper, nutmeg, egg and 1/2 cup beef broth. Cut pocket in each pork chop. Rub with salt, sage and thyme; stuff with dressing. Brush chops with oil. Place in large baking pan. Bake in preheated 450-degree oven for 30 minutes or until brown, turning chops once. Reduce oven temperature to 400 degrees; drain off fat from pan. Mix 1 cup water with remaining broth; pour over pork chops. Cover; bake for 50 to 60 minutes longer or until pork chops are tender. Place pork chops on platter; garnish with watercress and lemon slices. Pan juices may be thickened with cornstarch mixed with water, if desired.

EXTRA POINT PORK DINNER

4 pork chops
Flour
Salt and pepper to taste
4 potatoes, sliced
1 onion, sliced
1 can chicken gumbo soup

Dredge pork chops with flour. Saute in hot fat in skillet until browned; season with salt and pepper. Place sliced potatoes in casserole; add onion. Place pork chops on top; pour soup over pork chops. Pour a small amount of water in pan drippings; stir to mix well. Pour pan juices over pork chops. Bake, covered, in preheated 350-degree oven for 1 hour and 30 minutes or until done.

PORK CHOPS WITH CHERRIES

4 1/2-in. pork chops
1 tbsp. shortening

Recipes on pages 25 and 30.

Salt and pepper to taste
1 1-lb. 1-oz. can pitted light cherries
1/4 c. slivered almonds
6 whole cloves
1 tbsp. cider vinegar
Few drops of red food coloring (opt.)

Saute pork chops in shortening until brown; season with salt and pepper. Combine cherries with syrup, almonds, cloves, vinegar and food coloring; pour over pork chops. Cover; simmer for 30 minutes or until pork chops are tender. Yield: 4 servings.

ORIENTAL SPARERIBS

2 lb. spareribs
1 onion, chopped
1/3 clove of garlic, minced
2 tbsp. oil
1 tbsp. vinegar
1 tbsp. honey
1 tbsp. lemon juice
1 tsp. prepared mustard
1 tsp. salt
Pepper to taste
1/4 c. soy sauce
1/2 c. water

Cut spareribs into serving pieces; place in baking pan. Saute onion and garlic in oil in saucepan; stir in remaining ingredients. Pour over spareribs. Bake in preheated 325-degree oven for about 1 hour or until done, basting frequently.

ORANGE-GLAZED PORK

1 4-lb. pork loin
1 sm. onion, grated
1 tbsp. butter
2 tbsp. brown sugar
1 1/2 tsp. cornstarch
1/2 tsp. ground ginger
1 c. orange juice
1 tbsp. steak sauce

Place pork loin, fat side up, on rack in roasting pan. Bake in preheated 325-degree oven for 1 hour and 30 minutes. Saute onion in butter in saucepan until soft. Stir in remaining ingredients; cook, stirring constantly, until thick. Brush over pork loin; bake for 1 hour longer or until done, brushing every 15 minutes with onion mixture. Yield: 4 servings.

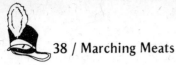

PORK ROAST COUNTERPOINT

1   3 1/2 to 4-lb. pork roast
Salt
Pepper to taste
1   8-oz. can tomato sauce
2 tbsp. lemon or lime juice
1 tsp. grated lemon rind
2 tbsp. brown sugar
1/2 tsp. nutmeg or allspice
1 No. 2 can pineapple chunks
1/2 c. seedless raisins

Sprinkle pork roast with salt to taste and pepper; place in baking pan. Bake in preheated 325-degree oven for 1 hour. Pour off excess fat. Combine tomato sauce, lemon juice, 1/2 cup water, lemon rind, 1/2 teaspoon salt, brown sugar and nutmeg in saucepan. Drain pineapple; reserve juice. Add reserved juice to tomato sauce mixture; stir well. Simmer for 10 minutes. Add raisins and pineapple chunks; pour over pork roast. Bake for about 2 hours longer or until done, basting occasionally and adding water, if needed. Yield: 6 servings.

HAM IN MUSHROOM SAUCE

2 tbsp. chopped onion
1 tbsp. butter or margarine
1 can cream of mushroom soup
1 c. shredded sharp cheese
1 tbsp. sherry (opt.)
1 c. diced cooked ham
2 tbsp. chopped pimento
1 tbsp. parsley
Patty shells

Saute onion in butter in saucepan until browned and tender. Blend in soup, cheese and sherry; cook over low heat until cheese is melted, stirring frequently. Add ham, pimento and parsley; heat thoroughly. Serve in patty shells. Peas may be added, if desired. Turkey or chicken may be substituted for ham.

HAM FONDUE CASSEROLE

3 c. cubed French bread
3 c. cubed cooked ham
3 1/2 c. cubed cheese
3 tbsp. flour
1 tbsp. dry mustard
3 tbsp. melted butter
4 eggs, beaten
3 c. milk
Several drops of hot sauce

Combine bread, ham and cheese in large bowl; mix well. Spread 1/3 of the mixture in layer in buttered rectangular 8-cup baking dish. Combine flour and mustard. Sprinkle 1 tablespoon flour mixture over ham layer; drizzle 1 tablespoon butter over top. Repeat process, making 2 additional layers. Combine eggs, milk and hot sauce; beat until foamy. Pour over ham mixture. Cover; let stand in refrigerator overnight. Bake, uncovered, in preheated 350-degree oven for 1 hour or until puffed and lightly browned. Serve immediately. Yield: 8 servings.

To prevent splashing when frying meat, sprinkle a little salt into the pan before adding the fat.

LINGUINE BOLOGNESE

1 egg
1 c. soft bread crumbs
2 c. ground cooked ham
2 tbsp. minced onion
1/2 tsp. dry mustard
1/2 tsp. pepper
2 tbsp. butter or margarine
1/2 c. chopped onion
1/2 c. chopped carrot
1/2 c. chopped celery
2   1-lb. cans tomatoes
1 tsp. salt
1/4 tsp. sugar
1 tsp. lemon juice
8 oz. linguine

Combine egg, bread crumbs and 1/4 cup water in large bowl; let stand for 5 minutes to soften bread crumbs. Add ham, minced onion, mustard and 1/4 teaspoon pepper; mix well. Shape into 1-inch balls. Melt butter in large skillet. Add ham balls; brown on all sides. Remove from skillet. Place chopped onion, carrot and celery in skillet, adding more butter, if needed. Saute vegetables for 10 minutes or until tender. Add tomatoes, salt, remaining 1/4 teaspoon pepper, sugar and lemon juice; simmer, uncovered, for 40 minutes. Add ham balls; heat through. Cook linguine according to package directions; place in chafing dish. Add ham balls and sauce. Yield: 4 servings.

Photograph for this recipe on page 35.

VEAL FIESTAS

1 1/2 lb. veal steak
Salt and pepper to taste
1/4 c. flour
1/4 c. shortening
3 lg. onions, sliced
1/2 c. chili sauce
1/2 c. grated cheese
1 1/2 c. cooked macaroni

Cut veal into serving pieces; season with salt and pepper. Dredge veal with flour. Saute on both sides in hot shortening in heatproof casserole; cover with onions, chili sauce and 1 1/2 cups hot water. Cover. Bake in preheated 375-degree oven for 30 minutes or until tender. Remove cover; sprinkle with cheese. Bake for 10 minutes longer or until cheese melts. Remove veal to hot platter. Stir macaroni into pan juices; heat through. Spoon macaroni mixture over veal. Yield: 4 servings.

VEAL VARIATION

3 lb. lean veal
1/2 c. flour
1 egg, well beaten
Bread crumbs
Butter or margarine
3/4 lb. mushrooms, cut in halves
1 onion, chopped
Salt and pepper to taste
Dash of mace
1/2 pt. (about) cream
1   1-lb. can green peas, drained
1/2 c. Parmesan cheese

Cut veal into 1/2 x 1/2 x 2-inch strips. Dredge with flour; dip in egg. Dredge with crumbs. Saute in small amount of butter until golden. Arrange veal in casserole; add mushrooms and onion. Season with salt, pepper and mace. Cover with cream. Bake in preheated 325-degree oven for 2 hours. Remove from oven. Add peas; sprinkle with cheese. Return to oven; bake for 30 minutes longer. Yield: 6 servings.

VEAL FRICASSEE IN PASTRY SHELLS

1 pkg. frozen pastry shells
1   2-lb. veal shoulder
Butter
2 tbsp. flour
1 tsp. salt
1 tbsp. lemon juice or white wine
1 tsp. capers
1 egg yolk
1 tbsp. heavy cream
8 oz. sliced mushrooms

Bake pastry shells according to package directions. Place veal in kettle in enough water to cover; boil until tender. Remove veal; reserve 2 cups stock. Cut veal into cubes; keep warm. Melt 2 tablespoons butter in top of double boiler; stir in flour and salt until smooth. Add reserved stock gradually; cook, stirring, until thickened. Stir in lemon juice and capers. Beat egg yolk and cream together. Add small amount of hot mixture to egg yolk mixture, blending well; return egg yolk mixture to double boiler. Cook for about 1 minute longer, stirring constantly. Remove from heat. Saute mushrooms in butter; stir mushrooms and veal into cream sauce. Fill pastry shells with veal mixture; serve immediately.

VEAL PARMIGIANA

4 veal cutlets, pounded
Seasoned flour
1 egg, beaten
Bread crumbs
Vegetable oil
1 pkg. sliced mozzarella cheese
1   8-oz. can tomato sauce
1/2 tsp. oregano
1/2 c. grated Parmesan cheese
Paprika to taste

Dredge cutlets with flour; shake off excess flour. Dip in egg; dredge with crumbs. Place on rack in pan; chill for at least 1 hour. Saute cutlets in 1/4 inch hot oil until browned. Place in shallow casserole; cover with mozzarella cheese. Combine tomato sauce and oregano in saucepan; bring to a boil. Pour over cutlets; sprinkle with Parmesan cheese, paprika and small amount of oil. Bake in preheated 350-degree oven for 30 minutes or until done.

Parading Poultry

Perfect for a picnic, a family dinner, an elegant occasion or for a lively banquet, poultry has long been an American favorite. The mild flavor of domestic poultry blends well with an almost unlimited choice of sauces, seasonings, and side dishes. The distinctive flavor of wild fowl (game birds) transforms an ordinary meal into a truly unique feast.

Poultry dishes can't be matched when it comes to feeding busy, bustling children — and their friends, teachers and parents for that matter! Chicken is one meat that is cheaper today than in the past, and a large turkey makes excellent use of even the tightest food dollar. They say there's one in every crowd, but who doesn't love a golden-roasted turkey? Try *Gridiron Barbecued Turkey* for a delicious change in the turkey-and-all-the-trimmings menu. And, for a special poultry entree, *Classic Country Captain* can't be beat. Or, as part of a hayride party on a chilly fall evening, serve the kids generous portions of *Turkey In The Straw.*

Use a variety of poultry in your menu — nutrition, flavor and economy will be your rewards. Band members and cheerleaders think your cooking will receive an excellent rating, too, when you serve some of their favorite poultry recipes.

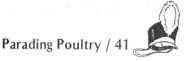

BARBECUED RHYTHM STICKS

1/4 c. catsup
2 tbsp. lemon juice
2 tbsp. soy sauce
1/4 c. salad oil
1/2 tsp. monosodium glutamate
12 chicken drumsticks

Combine all ingredients except chicken; mix well. Add chicken; stir until coated. Let stand at room temperature for 2 hours, spooning marinade over chicken occasionally. Remove drumsticks from marinade; reserve marinade. Place drumsticks in wire broiling basket. Grill over low coals for about 25 minutes, basting with reserved marinade occasionally. Turn; grill for 20 minutes longer or until tender, basting with marinade occasionally. Chicken may be marinated overnight in refrigerator, if desired. Yield: 6 servings.

BARBECUED LEMON CHICKEN

3 2 1/2 to 3-lb. chickens
1 c. salad oil
3/4 c. lemon juice
1 tbsp. salt
2 tsp. paprika
2 tsp. onion powder
1 tsp. garlic powder
2 tsp. crushed sweet basil
2 tsp. crushed thyme

Split chickens; remove wings and tails. Place in shallow pan. Combine remaining ingredients in jar. Cover; shake well to blend. Pour over chicken; cover tightly. Marinate for 12 hours or longer in refrigerator, turning chicken occasionally. Remove chicken from refrigerator 1 hour before grilling. Drain chicken; reserve marinade. Grill chicken over hot coals for about 20 minutes on each side or until done, basting frequently with reserved marinade. Serve with barbecue sauce, if desired. Yield: 6 servings.

TWIRLY BIRD BARBECUE

1 c. catsup
1/4 c. (packed) brown sugar
1/4 c. vinegar
1/4 c. A-1 sauce
1 tsp. chili powder

1 tsp. celery seed
2 tbsp. lemon juice
2 tbsp. minced onion
2 c. boiling water
2 2-lb. broilers, quartered

Mix all ingredients except broilers in saucepan; bring to a boil. Place broilers on grill over hot coals. Cook until chicken is tender and brown, turning and basting frequently with barbecue sauce. May be broiled in oven, if desired.

SUMMERTIME PICNIC CHICKEN

2 chickens, halved
Seasoned flour
Shortening
8 carrots
4 potatoes, quartered
4 lg. onions, quartered
Salt and pepper to taste
1 to 1 1/2 c. white wine

Cut heavy-duty aluminum foil into four 2-foot squares. Dredge chickens with seasoned flour; cook in hot shortening in heavy skillet until brown. Place 1 chicken half on each square of foil. Cut carrots into 2-inch slices. Arrange carrots, potatoes and onions around chicken on foil squares; season with salt and pepper. Pour wine into pan drippings in skillet; mix well. Spoon wine mixture over chicken and vegetables; seal foil squares tightly. Place in shallow baking pan. Bake in preheated 350-degree oven for 45 minutes or until chicken is tender. May be cooked over hot charcoal, if desired. One can cream of mushroom soup may be substituted for wine.

CHICKEN a la CAN CAN

1 can cream of chicken soup
1 can cream of celery soup
1 soup can water
1 1/2 c. diced cooked chicken
1 1/3 c. Minute rice
1 can French-fried onion rings

Combine soups, water and chicken in saucepan. Add rice; mix well. Bring to a boil over high heat; reduce heat. Cover; simmer for 7 minutes. Spoon into serving dish; top with onion rings. Yield: 4-6 servings.

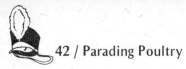

CLASSICAL CHICKEN CASSEROLE

1/3 c. flour
2 tsp. salt
1 tsp. paprika
6 chicken breast halves
1/4 c. butter
6 slices cooked ham
1 tsp. dried crumbled savory
12 celery leaves
1 c. canned sliced mushrooms
1/2 c. sauterne
1 c. sour cream

Combine flour, salt and paprika in paper bag; shake chicken breasts in bag, one at a time, until well floured. Cook chicken in butter in skillet over medium heat until brown. Place ham slices in 13 1/2 x 8 3/4 x 1 3/4-inch baking dish; sprinkle with savory. Place 2 celery leaves on each ham slice; cover with chicken. Arrange mushrooms over chicken. Pour sauterne into skillet in which chicken was browned; stir well. Mix remaining flour mixture with sour cream; stir into sauterne mixture. Pour over chicken; cover with lid or foil. Bake in preheated 350-degree oven for 1 hour. Mixing flour mixture with sour cream prevents curdling while baking. Yield: 6 servings.

CLASSIC COUNTRY CAPTAIN

8 chicken breasts
1 c. seasoned flour
1/2 c. shortening
2 onions, chopped
2 green peppers, chopped
1 clove of garlic, minced
1 tbsp. curry powder
1 1/2 tsp. salt
1/2 tsp. white pepper
1/2 tsp. thyme
2 cans tomatoes
1 tbsp. chopped parsley
6 c. hot cooked rice
1/4 c. currants
1/4 lb. toasted almonds

Remove skins from chicken; dredge chicken with flour. Fry in shortening in skillet until brown. Remove chicken from skillet; keep warm. Saute onions, green peppers and garlic in shortening remaining in skillet until onions are tender. Stir in curry powder, salt, pepper and thyme; mix well. Add tomatoes and parsley; heat through. Place chicken in large casserole; pour tomato sauce over chicken. Cover. Bake in preheated 350-degree oven for 45 minutes. Place rice in center of serving dish. Remove chicken from casserole; arrange around rice. Mix currants with sauce; pour over rice. Sprinkle almonds over chicken. Pecans may be substituted for almonds. Yield: 8 servings.

HIGH-STEPPING CHICKEN

1 3-lb. fryer
2 tsp. salt
1/2 tsp. garlic salt (opt.)
1 tsp. pepper
1 c. flour
1 c. shortening

Cut chicken into serving pieces; rub with salt. Sprinkle with garlic salt and pepper. Place flour in bag; shake chicken in flour to coat well. Cook chicken in shortening in heavy skillet over medium heat until brown on all sides. Reduce heat; cover. Cook until chicken is tender. Remove from skillet; drain on paper toweling.

CHICKEN PROVENCALE

3 lg. peeled tomatoes, seeded
2 2-lb. broilers, disjointed
Salt and pepper to taste
1/3 c. olive oil
Dry white wine
1 clove of garlic, minced
2 lg. onions, chopped
1/2 lb. mushrooms, sliced
2 tbsp. chopped parsley

Dice tomatoes. Sprinkle chicken with salt and pepper; cook in oil in skillet until brown. Reduce heat; pour 1/3 cup wine over chicken. Cover; simmer for 12 minutes. Add garlic and onions; cook until onions are tender. Stir in mushrooms and tomatoes; arrange vegetables over and around chicken. Cook, covered, until chicken is tender. Place chicken on hot serving platter. Add 1/2 cup wine to tomato mixture in skillet; blend well. Season with salt and pepper; stir in parsley. Pour over chicken; serve with buttered rice. Yield: 4 servings.

SOUTHERN CHICKEN AND DUMPLINGS

1 stewing hen
4 tsp. salt
Pepper to taste
3 c. all-purpose flour
1 tsp. baking powder
2 tbsp. shortening
Milk
3 tbsp. butter

Place hen in deep kettle; cover with water. Add 3 teaspoons salt and pepper; bring to a boil. Reduce heat; cover tightly. Simmer for at least 2 hours or until hen is very tender. Remove chicken from broth; cool. Remove chicken from bones; cut into large pieces. Mix flour, remaining 1 teaspoon salt and baking powder; cut in shortening. Stir in just enough milk to make stiff dough. Place on floured board; knead until very stiff. Roll out dough, 1/4 at a time, until paper-thin. Cut into 2-inch strips. Bring chicken broth to a boil. Add strips to broth, one at a time, so that broth continues to boil. Cook until dumplings are tender, adding boiling water, if needed, and stirring occasionally. Add chicken and butter; heat through.

FANCY CHICKEN LIVERS

1/3 c. butter
1 lb. chicken livers
1/4 c. finely chopped onion
1 tsp. salt
Dash of pepper
1 c. sliced mushrooms
1 tbsp. flour
1 c. half and half
4 baked patty shells
4 crisp bacon curls

Melt butter in skillet. Add chicken livers, onion, salt and pepper; cook over medium heat for 6 to 8 minutes, stirring frequently. Stir in mushrooms; cook for 4 minutes longer or just until livers are cooked through. Remove livers from skillet. Blend flour into skillet drippings; stir in half and half slowly. Cook, stirring constantly, until thickened. Return livers to skillet; heat through. Serve livers and sauce in patty shells; garnish with bacon curls. Livers may be served on toast, if desired. Yield: 4 servings.

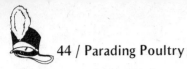

CHICKEN AND CORN BREAD DRESSING

1   5-lb. hen and giblets
Salt
4 c. corn bread crumbs
3 hard-boiled eggs
1 c. finely chopped celery
1 tsp. sage
5 biscuits, crumbled
1/4 c. minced onion
1/2 tsp. pepper
2 eggs, beaten
1/4 c. butter
1/4 c. flour

Place hen and giblets in kettle. Cover with water; add 1 1/2 tablespoons salt. Bring to a boil; reduce heat. Simmer until almost tender. Remove hen and giblets from broth; chop giblets. Place hen in baking pan. Bake in preheated 375-degree oven for 40 minutes or until well browned and tender. Bring chicken broth to a boil. Place corn bread crumbs in mixing bowl; add 3 cups chicken broth. Cover; let stand for 5 minutes. Chop 2 hard-boiled eggs. Add chopped eggs, celery, sage, biscuits, onion, pepper and beaten eggs to corn bread mixture; mix well. Add more broth, if needed; place in greased baking dish. Bake in preheated 375-degree oven for 1 hour. Chop remaining hard-boiled egg. Melt butter in saucepan. Add flour and 1/2 teaspoon salt; blend well. Add 2 cups chicken broth, giblets and chopped egg; cook until thick, stirring constantly. Serve with chicken and dressing.

PINEAPPLE SKEWERS PACIFICA

1   1-lb. 4-oz. can pineapple chunks
1/2 c. soy sauce
1/4 c. honey
1/4 c. cooking oil
1 tsp. dry mustard
1/3 c. wine vinegar
2 tbsp. minced fresh mint or green onion
1/2 c. catsup
2 lb. boned turkey breast, cubed

Drain pineapple; reserve 1/4 cup syrup. Combine reserved syrup, soy sauce, honey, oil, mustard, vinegar, mint and catsup; beat thoroughly until blended. Add turkey; mix well. Cover; let marinate in refrigera-

tor for 1 hour or longer. Thread turkey and pineapple chunks on skewers; brush with marinade. Broil until turkey is tender and glazed, brushing frequently with marinade. Water chestnuts, mushrooms, or tomato wedges may be added to turkey on skewers, if desired.

Photograph for this recipe on page 40.

TURKEY IN THE STRAW

2 tbsp. salad oil
1 c. chopped green pepper
1 c. chopped onion
1 clove of garlic, minced
2 tsp. salt
Pepper to taste
2 tsp. Worcestershire sauce
1/4 tsp. thyme or marjoram
3 c. water
1 1/2 c. uncooked rice
1 to 2 c. cooked diced turkey
1 to 2 c. cooked diced ham
1 sm. can mushrooms

Heat oil in skillet. Add green pepper, onion, and garlic; cook until tender. Stir in seasonings and water; simmer for 10 minutes. Add rice, turkey and ham; cover. Cook over low heat for 25 minutes or until rice is tender, adding boiling water, if needed. Add mushrooms with small amount of liquid; cook for about 5 minutes longer.

GRIDIRON BARBECUED TURKEY

1/4 c. vinegar
1/2 c. water
1 tbsp. salt
1/4 tsp. pepper
1/8 tsp. cayenne pepper
1 thick slice lemon
1 onion, sliced
1/4 c. butter or margarine
1 tbsp. Worcestershire sauce
1 1/2 tsp. liquid smoke
1   5-lb. turkey, quartered

Place first 9 ingredients in saucepan; mix well. Simmer for 20 minutes; stir in liquid smoke. Bring to a boil; remove from heat. Brush turkey generously with sauce; arrange, skin side up, on grill 5 to 8 inches above coals. Cook for 1 hour to 1 hour and 30 minutes, turning and brushing with sauce every 15 minutes.

BANQUET TURKEY WITH OYSTER DRESSING

Salt
1/2 tsp. pepper
4 tbsp. poultry seasoning
2 tbsp. ground sage
1 12-lb. turkey
2 stalks celery
2 lg. onions, quartered
1 loaf French bread, crumbled
1 lg. onion, diced
1/2 c. milk
1 pt. standard oysters and liquor
1/4 c. butter or margarine

Mix 1 tablespoon salt, 1/4 teaspoon pepper, 2 tablespoons poultry seasoning and 1 tablespoon sage. Rub outside and inside of turkey with seasoning mixture. Cut celery into 2-inch pieces; stuff turkey cavity with celery and quartered onions. Secure opening with skewers. Place turkey in roaster; cover with foil, securing tightly. Do not cover roaster. Bake in preheated 325-degree oven for 3 hours and 30 minutes to 4 hours or until turkey is brown and tender. Drain off pan drippings; reserve 1 cup for dressing. Combine bread crumbs, diced onion, 1 teaspoon salt and remaining seasonings. Add milk and oysters; mix well. Place in greased 9-inch square baking pan. Pour reserved drippings over dressing; dot with butter. Bake in preheated 400-degree oven for 30 minutes; serve with turkey. Yield: About 10 servings.

CORNISH HENS WITH PLUM SAUCE

4 Cornish hens, cut in halves
1 tsp. seasoned salt
2 lg. oranges, sliced
1/4 c. melted margarine
1/4 c. minced onion
1 tsp. ginger
1 tsp. Worcestershire sauce
1 1/2 tsp. prepared mustard
1/3 c. chili sauce
1/4 c. soy sauce
1 6-oz. can frozen lemonade, thawed
1 1-lb. can purple plums, drained and pureed
1/4 c. shredded coconut

Sprinkle hens with seasoned salt. Arrange orange slices in shallow roasting pan; place hens, skin side up, over oranges. Bake in preheated 350-degree oven for 45 minutes. Combine margarine, onion, ginger, Worcestershire sauce, mustard, chili sauce, soy sauce, lemonade and plum puree in saucepan; blend well. Simmer, stirring frequently, for 15 minutes; pour over hens. Bake for 20 minutes longer, basting frequently. Arrange hens on heated platter; top with plum mixture. Sprinkle with coconut.

DUCK a la ORANGE

1 4 to 5-lb. duck
1 tbsp. salt
1 orange
2 med. carrots
2 med. onions
2 celery stalks, cut in half
1 tbsp. instant chicken bouillon
1/2 c. water
1 can frozen unsweetened orange juice
1 tbsp. flour
1 tsp. Kitchen Bouquet
1/2 tsp. sugar

Rub outside and inside of duck with salt. Cut orange in half; remove seeds. Squeeze one of the halves into cavity of duck; place carrots, onions and celery in cavity. Place squeezed orange half in cavity; secure cavity with skewers or toothpicks. Pull neck skin over neck cavity; secure as for body cavity. Place duck on rack in roasting pan. Bake in preheated 325-degree oven for 2 hours; remove duck to shallow baking dish. Increase oven temperature to 350 degrees; bake duck for 1 hour longer. Pour off excess fat from roasting pan, leaving brown drippings. Add chicken bouillon, water, orange juice, flour, Kitchen Bouquet and sugar to drippings; bring to a full boil, stirring constantly. Reduce heat; simmer until consistency of syrup. Pour off fat from baking dish; spoon sauce over duck. Slice remaining orange half; place on duck. Bake for 15 to 20 minutes longer. Remove from oven; let stand for 10 minutes. Remove onion mixture from duck cavity before carving. Yield: 4-5 servings.

Syncopated Seafood

People everywhere, whether near the seacoast or far away, love to sit down to a delectable seafood dinner. And, because our lakes, rivers, streams and oceans are filled with an abundance of fish, families can enjoy many different kinds of fresh, frozen or canned seafood all yearlong. This great variety of shellfish and freshwater fish has resulted in an even greater variety of wonderful seafood recipes. Thanks to band members and cheerleaders from across the country, Syncopated Seafood offers some of the very best recipes you'll find anywhere!

To jazz up your next dinner party, serve *Dixieland Shrimp Creole.* It's an unusual kind of entree that is bound to be a hit. Or, for a delightfully different treat that will help you score with your family, try *Flounder Fantasia.* Even the children can have fun preparing *Solo Salmon,* a quick yet satisfying before-the-game dish.

To be sure, there's nothing better than the taste of tender, flaky morsels of fish. High in protein, it is both delicious and nutritious — a winning combination that can't be beat. Surprise your family tonight with any one of the following seafood dishes.

BROILED FRESHWATER BASS

4 freshwater bass
Paprika to taste
Salt and pepper to taste
1/4 c. butter

Cut bass to make 8 fillets. Place in broiler pan, skin side up. Brown under broiler; turn fillets. Sprinkle with paprika, salt and pepper. Dot with butter. Cover bottom of pan with small amount of water. Continue broiling until fish flakes easily.

FRIDAY FISH

Bass, well cleaned
Salt and pepper to taste
Cornmeal
Shortening

Sprinkle bass with salt and pepper; roll in cornmeal. Fry in shortening until golden brown; drain on paper towels.

CORN-CRISP CATFISH

1/2 c. evaporated milk
1 c. corn flake crumbs
1 tsp. monosodium glutamate
1 tsp. salt
1/4 tsp. pepper
1 1/2 lb. catfish steaks

Pour milk into bowl. Combine crumbs, monosodium glutamate, salt and pepper in another bowl. Dip steaks in milk; roll in crumb mixture. Arrange in shallow pan. Bake in preheated 375-degree oven for 20 minutes or until done.

FLOUNDER FANTASIA

2 1/2 lb. spinach
1 1/2 lb. flounder fillets
2 tbsp. finely chopped onion
Salt and pepper to taste
4 1/2 tbsp. butter
3 1/2 tbsp. flour
2 c. milk
12 whole cooked shrimp
1/4 c. grated sharp cheese

Cook spinach in small amount of boiling, salted water until tender. Drain and chop. Spread in ungreased 1 1/2-quart casserole. Place fillets on spinach; sprinkle onion over fillets. Season with salt and pepper. Melt butter; stir in flour. Add milk slowly; cook, stirring constantly, until thickened. Add salt and pepper; pour over onion. Arrange shrimp on top; sprinkle with cheese. Bake in preheated 400-degree oven for 20 minutes or until fish flakes easily. Yield: 4 servings.

FILLETS DIVAN

1 pkg. frozen broccoli
1 1-lb. package frozen fish fillets, thawed
1/2 c. grated American cheese
Salt
1/2 tsp. pepper
1/2 c. mayonnaise
1/4 c. finely chopped parsley
3 tbsp. pickle relish
1 tbsp. lemon juice
1 tsp. minced onion
2 egg whites

Cook broccoli according to package directions; drain. Arrange in single layer in a 9-inch square baking dish. Place fillets over broccoli. Sprinkle cheese, 1/2 teaspoon salt and pepper over fillets. Combine mayonnaise, parsley, relish, lemon juice, onion and salt to taste in small bowl. Beat egg whites until stiff peaks form; fold into mayonnaise mixture. Spread over fillets. Bake in preheated 400-degree oven for 30 minutes or until fillets are done and sauce is puffy and golden. Yield: 4 servings.

SWISS FISH

2 lb. frozen fish fillets, thawed
1 c. sour cream
1/2 c. grated Swiss cheese
1/4 c. finely chopped scallions or onion
3/4 tsp. salt
1/8 tsp. pepper
1 tsp. prepared mustard

Arrange fillets in baking pan. Combine remaining ingredients in small bowl; spread over fillets. Bake in preheated 375-degree oven for 20 minutes or until fish flakes easily when tested with fork. Place under broiler for 1 to 2 minutes to brown. Yield: 6 servings.

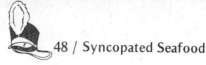

SALMONETTES HELOISE

1 15-oz. can pink salmon
1 egg
1/2 c. sifted flour
1 tsp. (heaping) baking powder

Drain juice from salmon into measuring cup; set aside. Add egg to salmon; mix well. Add flour; stir with fork. Mixture will be thick. Add baking powder to 1/4 cup salmon juice; beat with fork. Pour into salmon mixture; mix again with fork. Dip batter by spoonfuls, scooping out with another spoon into deep hot oil. Salmonettes will float on top of oil and turn themselves. Yield: 4-6 servings.

SOLO SALMON

1 can cream of celery soup
1/2 c. mayonnaise or salad dressing
1 egg, beaten
1/2 c. chopped onion
1/4 c. green pepper, chopped
1 16-oz. can salmon, drained and flaked
1 c. cracker crumbs

Combine all ingredients; place in greased loaf pan. Bake in preheated 350-degree oven for 1 hour. Yield: 8 servings.

SOUND-OFF SALMON CASSEROLE

1 1-lb. can salmon
1 4-oz. package egg noodles, cooked
1 med. onion, chopped
1/2 c. sliced pitted ripe olives
1 c. cheese soup
1 1/2 tsp. Worcestershire sauce
1 1-lb. can peas, drained

Drain salmon; reserve liquid. Flake the salmon. Combine noodles, onion, olives, soup, reserved liquid and Worcestershire sauce in a bowl. Add salmon and peas; mix lightly. Place in greased casserole. Bake in preheated 350-degree oven for about 30 minutes or until heated through.

GRILLED RED SNAPPER

1/2 c. butter or margarine
1/4 c. lemon juice
1 tbsp. Worcestershire sauce
1/4 tsp. onion salt
1 2-lb. red snapper
Chopped parsley

Melt butter slowly in 1-quart saucepan; add lemon juice, Worcestershire sauce and onion salt, mixing well. Remove from heat. Place snapper in hinged wire grill. Grill for 5 to 8 minutes on each side, basting occasionally with sauce. Turn only once. Heat remaining sauce; serve with fish. Sprinkle with parsley. Sauce may be used with other lean firm fish. Yield: 4 servings.

TUNA WITH CURRIED ALMOND-RICE

1 c. rice
8 tbsp. butter
1 can whole tomatoes, drained and chopped
1 clove of garlic, minced
1 tsp. Worcestershire sauce
4 drops of Tabasco sauce
1 tbsp. chopped parsley
1/4 tsp. paprika
1 tsp. salt
Dash of pepper
6 tbsp. flour
2 c. milk
1/2 c. white wine
2 9 1/4-oz. cans tuna, drained and rinsed
1/2 tsp. curry powder
1 c. blanched almonds

Place rice and 2 cups water in casserole; cover. Bake in preheated 350-degree oven for 1 hour. Melt 6 tablespoons butter in top of double boiler; add tomatoes, garlic, Worcestershire sauce, Tabasco sauce, parsley, paprika, salt and pepper. Cover; simmer for several minutes. Add flour; blend well. Add milk; cook, stirring constantly, until thickened. Add wine and tuna; keep warm over simmering water. Melt remaining butter in small frying pan; add curry powder and almonds. Cook over low heat, stirring, until almonds are brown; stir into rice. Serve tuna mixture over rice. Yield: 6 servings.

BAKED CLAMS WITH MUSHROOM SAUCE

1/2 c. minced onion
1/2 c. chopped mushrooms
1/4 c. butter
3 c. clams
1/4 tsp. paprika
1/2 tsp. salt
1/3 c. chopped parsley
1 to 1 1/2 c. medium white sauce
Buttered bread crumbs

Saute onion and mushrooms in butter until light brown; add clams. Cook for 5 minutes. Combine seasonings and white sauce; add clam mixture. Pour into greased casserole; sprinkle with crumbs. Bake in preheated 375-degree oven for 20 to 25 minutes. Yield: 6 servings.

WHITE CLAM SAUCE WITH SPAGHETTI

1/4 c. olive oil
1/4 c. butter
3 tbsp. minced green onions
2 tbsp. finely chopped parsley
2 cloves of garlic, pressed
1/8 tsp. white pepper
2   8-oz. cans minced clams
1/4 c. dry white wine

Combine olive oil and butter in saucepan; heat. Add green onions, parsley, garlic and pepper; saute without browning for 5 minutes or until onions are transparent. Drain clams; reserve juice. Stir clams into butter mixture; cook for 2 minutes. Add reserved juice and wine; simmer for 5 minutes. Serve over spaghetti or other pastas. Yield: About 2 1/2 cups.

CRAB CONCERTO

6 tbsp. butter
2 tbsp. finely chopped onion
1/2 c. finely chopped celery
3 tbsp. flour
3/4 tsp. salt
2 c. half and half
4 tbsp. sherry
1 egg, beaten
1/4 tsp. hot sauce
3 c. crab meat
2 tbsp. chopped parsley
1 1/2 c. fine bread cubes

Heat 4 tablespoons butter in saucepan. Add onion and celery; saute until onion is tender but not brown. Blend in flour and salt; add half and half and sherry gradually. Cook, stirring constantly, until mixture thickens and comes to a boil. Remove from heat; add small amount of sauce to egg gradually, stirring rapidly. Return egg mixture to sauce; mix well. Add hot sauce, crab meat and parsley. Turn into casserole. Melt remaining butter in skillet; add bread cubes, tossing well. Sprinkle over crab mixture. Bake in preheated 350-degree oven for 20 minutes. Garnish each serving with lemon twist and sprig of parsley. Yield: 6 servings.

SCALLOPED OYSTERS

1 pt. oysters
Butter
1/4 lb. saltines, crushed
3 tbsp. minced shallots
Salt and pepper to taste
Paprika to taste
1/2 c. heavy cream
1 tbsp. Worcestershire sauce
4 drops of hot sauce
1/4 c. dry white wine

Drain oysters; reserve 1/2 cup liquor. Butter a casserole generously. Place 1/4 of the saltines in casserole. Cover with 1/3 of the oysters; sprinkle with 1/3 of the shallots. Sprinkle with salt, pepper and paprika; dot with butter. Repeat layers twice; sprinkle with remaining saltines. Dot with butter. Combine reserved oyster liquor with the cream, Worcestershire sauce, hot sauce and wine; pour over top. Bake in preheated 400-degree oven for 30 minutes. Yield: 6 servings.

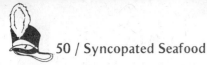
BAYOU JAMBALAYA

2 tbsp. butter
2 onions, chopped
1 tbsp. flour
1 1-lb. can tomatoes
1 green pepper, chopped
1 clove of garlic, chopped
1 tbsp. chopped parsley
Salt and pepper to taste
1 c. rice
1/4 tsp. thyme
1 bay leaf
2 c. chopped cooked ham
2 c. cooked shrimp
2 c. oysters and liquid

Melt butter in skillet; add onions. Cook over low heat until browned. Add flour gradually; stir until mixture is lightly browned. Add 2 cups water; cook, stirring constantly, until smooth and thickened. Add tomatoes, green pepper, garlic, parsley, salt, pepper, rice and herbs; cover. Simmer for 45 minutes or until rice is tender and small amount of liquid remains. Add ham, shrimp and oysters; cover. Simmer until edges of oysters are curled. Yield: 6 servings.

KEYNOTE FRIED SHRIMP

2 lb. jumbo shrimp
1 c. flour
1 tsp. baking powder
1 tsp. salt
2 eggs
1 c. milk
Cooking oil

Shell and devein shrimp; dry on toweling. Combine flour, baking powder, salt, eggs and milk in mixing bowl; beat vigorously. Dip shrimp into batter; fry in deep hot oil until golden brown.

SNAPPY SCAMPI

2 lb. large shrimp
1/2 c. butter
1/2 tsp. salt
3 cloves of garlic, crushed
2 tbsp. chopped parsley
1 tsp. grated lemon peel
1 tbsp. lemon juice

Shell and devein shrimp, leaving tails intact. Melt butter in 13 x 9 x 2-inch baking pan. Add salt, garlic and 1 tablespoon parsley; mix well. Arrange shrimp in single layer in baking dish. Bake in preheated 400-degree oven for 5 minutes. Turn shrimp; sprinkle with lemon peel, lemon juice and remaining parsley. Bake for 8 to 10 minutes longer. Arrange shrimp on heated platter. Pour butter mixture over shrimp. Garnish with lemon wedges. Serve immediately. Yield: 6 servings.

CHINESE SHRIMP WITH RIPE OLIVES

1 c. canned pitted California ripe olives
1 lb. shelled deveined shrimp
1 clove of garlic, crushed
1/4 tsp. powdered ginger
2 tbsp. oil
1/2 lb. ground lean pork
1/2 c. diagonally sliced celery
1 10 1/2-oz. can chicken broth
2 tbsp. cornstarch
2 tbsp. soy sauce
1/4 c. chopped green onion

Slice ripe olives diagonally. Saute shrimp with garlic and ginger in oil for 1 minute. Shape ground pork into small balls. Add to shrimp; cook for 2 to 3 minutes. Add celery and 1 cup broth; bring to boil. Cover; simmer for 10 minutes. Combine cornstarch with remaining broth and soy sauce; stir into shrimp mixture. Add ripe olives and green onion; cook, stirring, until sauce thickens. Serve with steamed rice. Two tablespoons dry sherry may be substituted for an equal amount of broth, if desired. Yield: 4 servings.

Photograph for this recipe on page 46.

DIXIELAND SHRIMP CREOLE

3 to 4 lb. shrimp
5 tbsp. shortening
1/4 c. flour
1 lg. onion, chopped
6 green onions, chopped
1/2 c. chopped green pepper
1/2 c. chopped celery
1 sm. clove of garlic, chopped
1 No. 303 can tomatoes

Salt and pepper to taste
Red pepper to taste
1/2 tsp. chopped parsley
1 bay leaf
1 tbsp. Worcestershire sauce

Shell and devein shrimp. Heat shortening in a deep heavy skillet. Add flour; cook, stirring, until browned. Add onion, green onions, green pepper, celery and garlic; stir in tomatoes. Season with salt, pepper, red pepper, parsley, bay leaf and Worcestershire sauce. Simmer, stirring frequently, for 30 minutes. Add shrimp; cook for 20 minutes longer. Serve over steamed rice.

C-SHARP SHRIMP NEWBURG

2 tbsp. butter
1 3/4 tbsp. flour
1 c. cream
3 tbsp. catsup
3/4 tsp. Worcestershire sauce

1 lb. cooked shrimp
1/2 c. mushrooms (opt.)
Salt, paprika and cayenne pepper to taste

Melt butter; stir in flour. Add cream slowly; cook, stirring constantly, until thick. Add catsup, Worcestershire sauce, shrimp and mushrooms; season with salt, paprika and cayenne pepper. Serve over hot rice. Yield: 4 servings.

BAKED SCALLOPS

2 lb. scallops
Parsley flakes
1/4 c. butter
Salt and pepper to taste

Arrange half the scallops in well-greased baking dish. Sprinkle with parsley flakes; dot with butter. Season with salt and pepper. Repeat layers; cover. Bake in preheated 325-degree oven for 45 minutes. Yield: 6 servings.

COQUILLE ST. JACQUES

6 tbsp. butter
3 tbsp. flour
1 tsp. salt
1/8 tsp. white pepper
2 c. light cream
1/4 c. finely chopped onions
1/2 lb. scallops, sliced
1/2 c. sliced mushrooms
3/4 lb. cooked shrimp
1/2 lb. crab meat
2 tbsp. sherry
5 tbsp. bread crumbs

Combine 4 tablespoons butter with flour, salt and white pepper in skillet; stir in cream gradually. Simmer, stirring constantly, until sauce is smooth and thickened. Saute onions in remaining butter in small skillet; add scallops. Saute for 5 minutes; remove onions and scallops. Add mushrooms; saute for 3 to 5 minutes. Combine shrimp, scallops, onions, crab meat, mushrooms and sherry with sauce; mix lightly. Place in individual baking dishes; sprinkle with crumbs. Bake in preheated 400-degree oven for 15 minutes or until heated through and crumbs are browned.

Virtuoso Vegetables

Crispy, colorful and chocked full of vitamins and minerals, vegetables add kaleidoscopic interest to hearty entrees and irresistible side dishes. No matter how they are served — raw or cooked, plain or fancy — vegetables offer a world of flavors and are always good for you. Of course, vegetables are tastiest when they are fresh and in season. But, because they are available all year-round either frozen or canned, they are always a good buy.

Served with a fruit salad and crunchy rolls, *Stuffed Cabbage Cartwheels* make an entire meal. *Corn On The Coals* is perfect (no mess to clean up!) for a cookout. For a colorful dish, serve *Deviled Peas Potpourri*. And, for a surprise with a one-of-a-kind taste, try *Ratatouille Rhythm*.

Although young people are not known for their love of vegetables, they will be as delighted with these recipes as anyone could be. Everyone loves the same old thing when it is prepared in a brand new way. Just like bands and cheerleaders are for teams everywhere, vegetables are the spirit behind a winning meal.

ASPARAGUS AND ALMOND ALLEGRO

1   10-oz. package frozen asparagus
1/2 c. slivered blanched almonds
6 tbsp. butter
3 tbsp. flour
1 c. milk
1 c. light cream
3/4 tsp. salt
Dash of pepper
2 c. instant rice

Cook asparagus according to package directions; drain. Saute almonds in 4 tablespoons butter in saucepan until brown, stirring constantly; remove almonds from saucepan. Blend flour into pan drippings; add milk gradually, stirring constantly. Add cream, salt and pepper; cook over low heat until thickened, stirring constantly. Add asparagus and almonds; mix gently. Prepare rice according to package directions. Add remaining 2 tablespoons butter; toss lightly. Place rice in serving dish; spoon asparagus mixture over rice. Yield: 6 servings.

FRENCH-STYLE GREEN BEANS

2 lb. fresh green beans
1 sm. clove of garlic, crushed
1/4 c. butter
2 tsp. salt
1/8 tsp. pepper
2 tsp. finely chopped parsley

Remove ends and strings from beans. Place beans, one at a time, on chopping board. Cut through each bean lengthwise, halfway between string sides, with sharp paring knife. Wash beans; place in top of vegetable steamer. Pour water into base of steamer pan to just below level of top of steamer pan; bring to a boil. Add beans; cover. Cook for 30 minutes or until beans are crisp-tender. Remove top steamer pan from base. Pour water from base of steamer pan; turn beans into base. Add garlic, butter, salt, pepper and parsley; mix well. Serve immediately. Beans may be cooked in colander over large saucepan of boiling water, if steamer pan is not available. Yield: About 6 servings.

RAH RAH MIXED BEAN CASSEROLE

1 1/2 lb. ground beef
1/2 c. catsup

1/2 tsp. dry mustard
2 tbsp. vinegar
3 tbsp. dark brown sugar
1 sm. onion, minced
1   1-lb. can green lima beans, drained
1   1-lb. can red kidney beans, drained
1   1-lb. can pork and beans
1/2 tsp. salt

Cook beef in skillet until brown; mix with remaining ingredients. Place in 2 greased 1 1/2-quart casseroles. Bake in preheated 350-degree oven for 30 minutes.

BOSTON BAKED BEANS

2 c. navy or pea beans
1 onion, chopped
1/2 lb. salt pork
2 tsp. salt
1/4 tsp. dry mustard
Pinch of pepper
1/4 c. molasses

Soak beans in 2 quarts warm water in large kettle for 2 hours. Bring to a boil; reduce heat. Simmer until tender; drain, reserving water. Fill bean pot with half the beans; add onion. Add remaining beans. Remove rind from salt pork; cut salt pork at intervals with knife. Press pork into beans. Combine salt, mustard, pepper, molasses and 3/4 cup boiling water; pour over beans. Add enough reserved water to cover beans; cover bean pot. Bake in preheated 300-degree oven for 3 hours. Remove cover; bake for 1 hour longer. Yield: 6 servings.

VAGABOND RAISIN BAKED BEANS

1/2 c. California seedless raisins
1 sm. onion
1 tart apple, peeled and cored
1/2 c. chopped ham
1   1-lb. 15-oz. can baked beans
1 1/2 tsp. dry mustard
1/4 c. sweet pickle relish
1/2 c. catsup or chili sauce

Chop raisins, onion and apple fine. Combine all ingredients; turn into bean pot or casserole. Bake, covered, in preheated 300-degree oven for 1 hour and 30 minutes to 2 hours or until done. Yield: About 1 quart.

Photograph for this recipe on page 52.

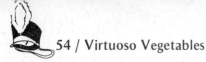

BROCCOLI AND COTTAGE CHEESE DISH

    1 10-oz. box frozen chopped broccoli
    1 c. creamed cottage cheese
    2 eggs, slightly beaten
    1/4 tsp. salt
    1 tsp. seasoned salt
    1/4 tsp. pepper
    1/4 tsp. steak sauce
    1 tsp. instant minced onion
    1/4 c. melted butter
    1/4 c. soft bread crumbs

Cook broccoli according to package directions; drain. Add remaining ingredients except butter and bread crumbs; mix well. Place in small, shallow baking dish. Mix butter and crumbs; sprinkle over broccoli mixture. Bake in preheated 350-degree oven for 30 minutes. Yield: 4 servings.

FRESH BROCCOLI WITH MILD CHEESE SAUCE

    1 bunch fresh broccoli
    1 tsp. salt
    1/8 tsp. pepper
    2 tbsp. butter or margarine
    2 tbsp. flour
    1 c. milk
    1 c. shredded American cheese

Wash broccoli; remove large leaves and tough part of stalks. Separate flowerets or cut into individual spears. Place in large saucepan; cover with 1/2 inch boiling water. Add salt and pepper; simmer, covered, for 10 to 12 minutes or until crisp-tender. Melt butter in saucepan; blend in flour. Stir in milk; cook, stirring constantly, until sauce thickens and comes to a boil. Add cheese; cook, stirring, until cheese is melted. Drain broccoli well; serve with cheese sauce.

Photograph for this recipe on page 18.

STUFFED CABBAGE CARTWHEELS

    Cabbage leaves
    1 lb. ground beef
    1 c. rice
    1/4 c. butter
    1 sm. can tomato sauce
    2 tsp. salt
    1 tsp. red pepper
    1 tsp. cinnamon
    Mint leaves
    1 16-oz. can tomatoes
    Juice of 1 lemon

Place cabbage leaves in boiling water; let stand until wilted. Drain. Mix beef, rice, butter, tomato sauce, salt, red pepper and cinnamon in bowl; place 2 heaping tablespoons beef mixture in each cabbage leaf. Roll up firmly; secure with wooden picks. Cover bottom of large saucepan with mint leaves. Arrange cabbage rolls close together over mint leaves; cover with tomatoes. Bring to a boil; reduce heat. Cover. Simmer for 45 minutes, adding water, if needed. Sprinkle with lemon juice; simmer for 15 to 20 minutes longer or until rice is done. Yield: 4-6 servings.

CABBAGE-CHEESE CASSEROLE

    1 2 1/2-lb. cabbage, shredded
    3 tbsp. butter
    3 tbsp. flour
    1 tsp. salt
    1 tsp. dry mustard
    1 c. evaporated milk
    2 c. grated Cheddar cheese
    3 tbsp. melted butter
    2 c. dry bread crumbs

Cook cabbage in boiling water until just tender. Drain; reserve 1/2 cup liquid. Melt butter in saucepan; stir in flour, salt and mustard. Add reserved liquid, milk and cheese; cook, stirring, until cheese melts. Place 1/3 of the cabbage in casserole. Pour 1/3 of the cheese sauce over cabbage; repeat layers 2 more times. Mix melted butter with crumbs; sprinkle over cabbage mixture. Bake in preheated 350-degree oven for 30 minutes.

MARVELOUS MARINATED CARROTS

    12 lg. carrots, sliced
    1 onion, chopped
    1/2 c. salad oil
    1 can tomato soup
    1 tsp. Worcestershire sauce
    3/4 c. sugar
    1/3 c. vinegar

1 tsp. salt
1 tsp. pepper
1 tsp. paprika
1 tsp. dry mustard

Cook carrots in boiling water until crisp-tender; drain. Place in large container. Mix remaining ingredients. Add to carrots; stir well. Cover container; refrigerate for 24 hours. Heat in double boiler before serving. May be served cold as appetizer.

If you add a little milk to water in which cauliflower is cooking, the cauliflower will remain attractively white.

AMERICAN CAULIFLOWER AU GRATIN

1 sm. cauliflower
3 tbsp. instant tapioca
3/4 tsp. salt
1/8 tsp. paprika
2 c. milk
1 c. grated American cheese
1 c. bread crumbs

Break cauliflower into flowerets. Cook in boiling, salted water until tender; drain. Place in greased casserole. Combine tapioca, salt, paprika and milk in heavy saucepan. Cook until thickened, stirring frequently; remove from heat. Add cheese; stir until melted. Pour over cauliflower; cover with crumbs. Bake in preheated 350-degree oven for 20 minutes. Yield: 6 servings.

SENSATIONAL CELERY

4 c. sliced celery
1 6-oz. can water chestnuts
1/2 c. canned mushroom stems and pieces
1/4 c. slivered blanched almonds
6 tbsp. butter
6 tbsp. flour
1/2 c. milk
1 can chicken broth or consomme
1 c. dry bread crumbs or Ritz cracker crumbs
1/2 c. grated Parmesan cheese

Cook celery in boiling water for 5 minutes; drain. Drain water chestnuts; reserve liquid. Slice water chestnuts. Drain mushrooms; reserve liquid. Mix celery, water chestnuts, almonds and mushrooms. Melt butter in saucepan. Add flour; stir until smooth. Add reserved liquids, milk and broth; cook, stirring, until thickened. Stir in celery mixture; pour into casserole. Top with crumbs; sprinkle with cheese. Bake in preheated 375-degree oven until bubbly and brown. Yield: 6 servings.

CORN ON THE COALS

6 ears of corn, unhusked
Salt to taste
Butter

Turn husks back from corn; remove silks. Trim tops from ears of corn; turn husks back over corn. Soak corn in enough water to cover for 2 hours. Remove corn from water; place over hot charcoal. Roast until husks are well browned. Remove husks from corn; serve corn with salt and butter.

EGGPLANT ENCORE

1 1 1/2-lb. eggplant
1 c. dry bread crumbs
2 c. grated Parmesan cheese
2 eggs
Cooking oil
1 lb. hamburger
Salt and pepper to taste
Garlic salt to taste
3 8-oz. cans tomato sauce
2 tsp. oregano
2 c. grated mozzarella cheese

Pare eggplant, if desired; cut into 1/4-inch slices. Mix bread crumbs and 1/2 cup Parmesan cheese; beat eggs with 2 tablespoons water until mixed. Dip eggplant slices into eggs; coat with crumb mixture. Cook, several slices at a time, in small amount of oil in skillet until brown, adding oil as needed; drain on paper towels. Drain oil from skillet; cook hamburger in skillet until brown. Stir in salt, pepper, garlic salt and tomato sauce; remove from heat. Place alternate layers of eggplant, remaining Parmesan cheese, oregano, hamburger mixture and mozzarella cheese in large baking dish. Bake in preheated 350-degree oven for 30 minutes or until bubbly and cheese is melted. Yield: 4-6 servings.

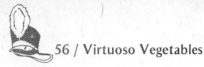

BAKED MUSHROOMS IN CHEESE SAUCE

8 lg. mushrooms
2 thick slices salt pork, diced
3 tbsp. butter
3 tbsp. flour
2 c. milk
3/4 tsp. salt
1/4 tsp. white pepper
1 c. grated Romano cheese
1/3 c. finely minced green onions
1 1/2 c. fine bread crumbs

Remove stems from mushrooms; chop coarsely. Cook salt pork in saucepan over low heat until all fat is rendered; remove pork from saucepan. Add chopped mushrooms to saucepan; cook over medium heat until all fat is absorbed. Set aside. Melt butter in top of double boiler over boiling water; stir in flour until smooth. Add milk gradually, stirring constantly; cook until thick, stirring frequently. Stir in salt and pepper. Add 3/4 cup cheese; stir until cheese is melted. Stir in onions and chopped mushrooms. Arrange mushroom caps, round side down, in shallow 9 1/2-inch baking dish; pour cheese sauce over mushrooms. Sprinkle bread crumbs over cheese sauce; sprinkle remaining 1/4 cup cheese evenly over bread crumbs. Bake in preheated 350-degree oven for about 20 minutes or until lightly browned. Parmesan or any hard cheese may be substituted for Romano cheese.

DEVILED PEAS POTPOURRI

1 sm. can pimentos
1 1-lb. 4-oz. can English peas, drained
1 green pepper, minced
1 c. grated cheese
1 tsp. Worcestershire sauce
1 sm. can mushrooms, drained
1 can cream of tomato soup
1 c. finely chopped celery
1/2 c. chili sauce
6 hard-cooked eggs, sliced
1 1/2 c. thick white sauce
Buttered bread crumbs (opt.)

Drain pimentos; chop. Combine with remaining ingredients. except eggs, white sauce and crumbs. Arrange layers of peas mixture, eggs and sauce in greased casserole; cover with bread crumbs. Bake in preheated 350-degree oven for 20 to 30 minutes. One can cream of mushroom soup may be used instead of white sauce.

Use greased muffin tins as molds when baking stuffed green peppers.

QUICK AND EASY ONION TARTLETS

1 1/2 c. finely chopped onions
1/4 tsp. Italian seasoning
1/4 c. butter or margarine
1/3 c. bleu cheese
12 3-in. unbaked pastry shells
3 lg. eggs, slightly beaten
1 c. light cream
1/2 tsp. salt
1/8 tsp. pepper

Saute onions with Italian seasoning in butter until onions are tender. Remove from heat. Add cheese; stir until cheese is melted. Spoon onion mixture evenly into pastry shells. Combine eggs, cream, salt and pepper; spoon over onion mixture. Bake in preheated 425-degree oven for 15 minutes. Reduce oven temperature to 350 degrees; bake for 20 minutes longer or until set.

CHEESY CREAMED ONIONS

18 to 20 sm. onions
2 c. water
1 1/2 tsp. salt
1/4 c. melted butter
1/4 c. flour
1 1/2 c. milk
1 c. grated cheese
1/2 c. chopped pecans

Combine onions, water and 1 teaspoon salt in 1 1/2-quart saucepan. Bring to a boil over high heat; reduce heat. Cover. Simmer for 15 minutes or until tender; drain. Melt butter in saucepan; stir in flour. Stir in milk and remaining 1/2 teaspoon salt; cook over medium heat, stirring constantly, until thickened. Add cheese; cook, stirring, until melted. Stir in onions; heat through. Turn into serving dish; sprinkle with pecans. Yield: 4-6 servings.

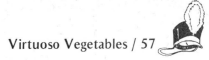

BUNDLED POTATO BATONS

6 med. potatoes, cut in strips
1 lg. onion, sliced
6 tbsp. butter
Salt and pepper to taste
Caraway seed to taste (opt.)

Place potatoes on large piece of double-folded aluminum foil; top with onion. Dot with butter; add salt and pepper. Sprinkle with caraway seed. Wrap loosely; seal tightly. Grill about 5 inches from coals for 20 minutes. Turn; grill for 20 minutes longer or until done. May be served with sour cream.

PLUPERFECT POTATOES

1 lg. package frozen hashed brown potatoes
1 can cream of celery soup
1 can cream of potato soup
1 c. sour cream
2 tbsp. chopped onion
3 tbsp. chopped green pepper
1 tsp. salt
1/4 tsp. pepper
Chopped parsley to taste
Paprika

Thaw hashed brown potatoes. Combine all ingredients except paprika in large bowl; place in greased 9 x 13-inch baking pan. Sprinkle with paprika. Bake in preheated 300-degree oven for 1 hour and 30 minutes or until potatoes are done.

RATATOUILLE RHYTHM

1 med. eggplant
1 lg. red sweet pepper
4 med. tomatoes
3 sm. zucchini
1/3 c. olive oil
2 med. onions, finely chopped
2 sm. cloves of garlic, pressed
2 tsp. minced parsley
1 1/2 tsp. salt
1/4 tsp. pepper
1 tsp. sugar

Trim stem from eggplant; do not peel. Cut eggplant into 1/2-inch slices; cut into cubes. Place eggplant in bowl with enough salted water to cover; weight eggplant down with plate. Let soak for at least 15 minutes. Remove seeds and membranes from sweet pepper; chop sweet pepper coarsely. Peel tomatoes; chop coarsely. Cut ends from zucchini; cut zucchini crosswise into thin slices. Heat oil in Dutch oven until sizzling. Add onions, sweet pepper and zucchini; cover. Cook for 5 minutes, stirring occasionally. Combine garlic and parsley; stir into onion mixture. Drain eggplant thoroughly; stir into zucchini mixture. Cover; cook for 5 minutes. Add tomatoes, salt, pepper and sugar; mix thoroughly. Cover; cook for 5 to 10 minutes longer or until almost all liquid has evaporated. Serve hot. One 1-pound can solid-pack tomatoes may be substituted for fresh tomatoes.

SQUASH SONATA

3 lb. yellow squash, sliced
2 onions, chopped
2 carrots, sliced
2 cans cream of chicken soup
1 carton sour cream
1 sm. jar pimentos
1/2 c. melted butter
1 pkg. herb-seasoned stuffing mix

Cook squash, onions and carrots in boiling, salted water until tender; drain well. Add soup and sour cream. Drain pimentos; chop. Add to squash mixture; stir well. Mix butter and stuffing mix; spread half the stuffing in greased casserole. Add squash mixture; cover with remaining stuffing mix. Bake in preheated 375-degree oven for 45 minutes.

VEGETABLE TRIO

1 1-lb. can lima beans
1 1-lb. can French-style green beans
1 1-lb. can green peas
1 c. mayonnaise
1 tbsp. prepared mustard
1 tbsp. Worcestershire sauce
1 med. onion, grated
2 hard-boiled eggs, chopped
1 can French-fried onion rings

Drain beans and peas; place in casserole. Mix remaining ingredients except onion rings. Add to bean mixture; stir until mixed. Place onion rings over top. Bake in preheated 350-degree oven for 20 minutes or until heated through. Bread crumbs may be used instead of onion rings.

Sound-Off Side Dishes

Mealtime is what you make it. So, why not make it as excitingly different as possible? Side dishes are something you can count on to bring just the right "lift" to breakfast, lunch or dinner. Just think of all the ways you can use ingredients such as eggs, noodles, cheese and rice to concoct super side dishes such as casseroles, dressings and omelets! Besides providing the nourishment your family needs, side dishes offer young and old alike the something extra they've been asking for.

For example, cheering will be all you'll hear once you serve *Two Bits-Four Bits Barley Casserole,* an unusual dish that probably few have ever tasted. And, while cheese has always been a favorite, *Strutter's Cheese Strata* makes a wonderful, new cheesy addition to any meal. Another ideal accompaniment is *First Down Chestnut Dressing.* It's at its very best when served with chicken or turkey.

Band members and cheerleaders know how much they like coming home from afternoon practice to the tantalizing aroma of a new dish being cooked. Thanks to this superb collection of Sound-Off Side Dish recipes, mealtime can always be enjoyable for you and your family.

EGGS BENEDICT

4 tsp. soft butter
2 English muffins, split
4 slices Canadian bacon or ham
6 c. water
1 tbsp. vinegar
4 eggs
Hollandaise Sauce

Spread butter on muffins; toast until brown. Broil Canadian bacon until done; place on toasted muffins. Bring water and vinegar to a boil in a stainless steel skillet. Drop eggs into skillet; reduce heat. Poach eggs until of desired doneness. Place poached eggs over bacon; cover with Hollandaise Sauce.

Hollandaise Sauce

3 egg yolks
1 tsp. lemon juice
1/4 tsp. salt
Pinch of pepper
1/2 c. butter

Place egg yolks in blender; blend until light and thick. Add lemon juice, salt and pepper. Melt butter; add to egg mixture very slowly while blending.

EGGS POACHED IN CHEESE SAUCE

2 tbsp. butter
2 tbsp. flour
3/4 tsp. salt
1/4 tsp. paprika
1 1/2 c. milk
1/4 tsp. Worcestershire sauce
1 c. grated cheese
6 eggs
2 tomatoes
6 pieces of toast

Melt butter; add flour, salt and paprika. Mix until smooth. Add milk gradually, stirring constantly. Cook until thick and smooth. Add Worcestershire and cheese; stir until melted. Pour into shallow pan; drop eggs into sauce. Poach over low heat until eggs are set. Cut each tomato into 3 slices; season. Place under broiler for several minutes. Place tomato slice on toast; top with poached egg. Pour sauce over top. Yield: 6 servings.

FRENCH OMELETTE

6 eggs, separated
1/2 c. milk
Salt and pepper to taste
2 sprigs of fresh or 1 tsp. dried parsley
1 lg. can mushrooms, drained
1 c. grated Swiss cheese

Beat egg whites until stiff but not dry. Place yolks, milk, salt, pepper, parsley, mushrooms and cheese in blender. Blend for 15 seconds. Fold yolk mixture into beaten whites. Pour into large buttered skillet. Bake in preheated 300-degree oven for 40 minutes or until golden brown and puffed. Yield: 4 servings.

OMELET ITALIANO

1 sm. can tomato sauce
1 tsp. Italian spice mix
1/2 tsp. oregano
1/2 tsp. sweet basil
6 lg. eggs
Salt and pepper to taste
1 4-oz. package grated mozzarella cheese
1 tbsp. butter or margarine

Combine sauce, spice mix, oregano and basil; simmer while omelet is cooking. Beat eggs lightly with salt and pepper. Stir in cheese. Melt butter in frypan over low heat. Pour egg mixture into pan; cook until edges brown. Fold omelet over; cook until set. Pour sauce over individual omelet servings. Yield: 4 servings.

SUPEROCTIVE SCRAMBLED EGGS

1/2 c. coarsely ground ham
6 eggs
1/4 tsp. Beau Monde seasoning
1/4 tsp. Worcestershire sauce
1/4 tsp. mustard
1/8 tsp. garlic powder
1/4 tsp. salt

Cook ham in electric frypan set at 340 degrees for 1 minute; reduce temperature to 300 degrees. Combine eggs, 6 tablespoons water and seasonings, beating at low speed of electric mixer for 1 minute. Pour egg mixture over ham. Cook, folding firm eggs over, until entire mixture is firm but not dry. Turn out onto warm serving plate; garnish with parsley.

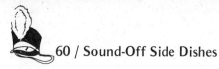

GOLDEN PUFF

32 saltines
3/4 lb. cheese slices
3 tbsp. chopped onion
2 1/2 c. milk
4 eggs, beaten
1/2 tsp. dry mustard
Dash of pepper

Arrange half the saltines in 12 x 8-inch baking dish. Cover with cheese slices and onion. Top with remaining saltines. Combine milk, eggs and seasonings; pour over crackers. Chill for at least 1 hour. Bake in preheated 325-degree oven for 40 minutes.

QUICHE LORRAINE

1 pkg. pastry mix
12 slices lean bacon
4 eggs
2 c. heavy cream
3/4 tsp. salt
1/8 tsp. powdered nutmeg
1/8 tsp. sugar
1/16 tsp. cayenne pepper
1/8 tsp. pepper
1 tbsp. softened butter or margarine
1/4 lb. Swiss cheese, grated

Prepare pastry according to package directions; fit into 9-inch pie plate. Chill for about 30 minutes. Fry bacon until crisp; drain on paper towels. Crumble. Beat eggs with cream, salt, nutmeg, sugar, cayenne pepper and pepper. Rub pie shell with butter. Sprinkle bacon and cheese into pie shell; pour egg mixture over bacon mixture. Bake in preheated 425-degree oven for 15 minutes. Reduce temperature to 300 degrees; bake for 40 minutes longer or until knife inserted in center comes out clean. Remove from oven; let stand for 5 minutes. Cut into wedges; serve at once.

STRUTTER'S CHEESE STRATA

Butter
8 slices bread, crusts removed
1 lb. sharp Cheddar cheese, grated
6 eggs, beaten
3 c. milk
3/4 tsp. salt
3/4 tsp. dry mustard
Dash of cayenne pepper

Butter both sides of bread slices. Arrange alternate layers of cheese and bread in buttered 8-inch square casserole. Combine eggs, milk, salt, mustard and cayenne pepper; pour over cheese and bread. Refrigerate overnight. Bake in preheated 350-degree oven for 1 hour. Yield: 4-6 servings.

THREE-CHEESE TORTILLA CASSEROLE

12 corn tortillas
3 tbsp. cooking oil
2 lg. white onions, sliced
1 8-oz. can tomato sauce
1 tbsp. oregano
1 tsp. salt
1/2 tsp. pepper
1 10-oz. can enchilada sauce
1/2 c. grated Parmesan cheese
2/3 lb. Jack cheese, shredded
1 pt. sour cream
1 c. shredded Cheddar cheese
1/2 tsp. paprika

Cut each tortilla into 8 pieces. Fry in heated oil until slightly crisp; drain. Saute onions in 1 teaspoon oil until wilted. Add tomato sauce, oregano, salt, pepper and enchilada sauce. Simmer for 10 minutes. Arrange alternate layers of tortilla pieces, tomato sauce, Parmesan cheese, Jack cheese and sour cream in greased 2-quart casserole, ending with sour cream. Bake in preheated 325-degree oven for 20 minutes. Sprinkle Cheddar cheese and paprika over top. Bake for 10 minutes longer.

TWO BITS-FOUR BITS BARLEY CASSEROLE

3/4 lb. fresh mushrooms
1/2 c. butter, melted
2 med. onions, chopped
1 1/2 c. barley
1 4-oz. jar pimento strips
1/4 tsp. salt
1/8 tsp. pepper
3 c. beef bouillon

Trim mushrooms; slice. Combine butter, onions and mushrooms in skillet; cook until onions are golden and mushrooms are tender. Add barley; cook until lightly browned. Place in 1 1/2-quart casserole. Chop pimento strips. Add pimento, salt, pepper and 2 cups bouillon; cover. Bake in preheated 350-degree oven for 45 minutes. Add remaining bouillon. Bake for 30 minutes longer. Yield: 6-8 servings.

PICCOLO PILAF

1/2 c. butter or margarine
2 c. long grain rice
1 tsp. salt
1/4 tsp. saffron
Freshly ground pepper
3　10 1/2-oz. cans beef consomme
2 med. onions, peeled and thinly sliced
1 c. dark seedless raisins

Melt 1/4 cup butter in heavy skillet. Add rice; cook over low heat until golden brown, stirring occasionally. Add seasonings and consomme; cover. Bake in preheated 325-degree oven for 1 hour and 30 minutes. Cook onions in remaining 1/4 cup butter over very low heat until soft and yellow. Stir raisins into rice; let stand for 5 minutes. Mound raisin rice on serving platter; garnish with onion rings. Yield: 6 servings.

GREEN RICE CASSEROLE

4 c. cooked rice
2 c. grated Cheddar cheese
1 1/2 c. finely chopped parsley
2 tbsp. chopped onion
6 eggs, separated
Butter
Salt and pepper to taste
3 tbsp. flour
1 1/2 c. milk
2 sm. cans mushrooms

Combine rice, cheese, parsley, onion, egg yolks and 1/2 cup melted butter in mixing bowl. Season with salt and pepper; fold in stiffly beaten egg whites. Pour into greased 2-quart baking dish. Bake in preheated 350-degree oven for 30 to 45 minutes. Melt 2 tablespoons butter in saucepan; stir in flour to make a smooth paste. Add milk gradually, stirring until well blended. Cook for 5 minutes or until sauce is thick, stirring constantly. Stir in mushrooms; heat thoroughly. Serve over rice mixture. Yield: 12 servings.

LARGO SEASHELLS

1　16-oz. box seashell macaroni
1 lg. onion, diced
1 tbsp. diced green pepper
1/2 c. butter or margarine
Salt to taste
1　1-pt. carton cottage cheese

Cook macaroni according to package directions; drain. Saute onion and green pepper in butter until tender; add macaroni. Season with salt; stir in cottage cheese. Serve immediately.

FIRECRACKER MACARONI AND CHEESE

Salt
4 to 6 qt. boiling water
4 c. elbow macaroni
1 med. onion, chopped
1/2 c. chopped celery
1/3 c. butter or margarine
1/3 c. flour
2 1/4 c. milk
1 c. heavy cream
1 tsp. crushed red pepper
1 tsp. Worcestershire sauce
4 c. grated sharp Cheddar cheese
1/2 c. dry white wine

Stir 2 tablespoons salt into rapidly boiling water. Add macaroni gradually so that water continues to boil. Cook, uncovered, until tender, stirring occasionally. Drain in colander. Saute onion and celery in butter in medium saucepan until crisp-tender. Stir in flour; stir in milk and cream. Bring to a boil; boil for 1 minute, stirring constantly. Remove from heat. Add 1 teaspoon salt, pepper, Worcestershire sauce and 3 cups cheese; stir until cheese melts. Add wine gradually. Combine macaroni and cheese sauce; turn into 3-quart baking dish. Sprinkle remaining 1 cup cheese on top. Bake, uncovered, in preheated 375-degree oven for 15 to 20 minutes or until bubbly. Yield: 8 servings.

Photograph for this recipe on page 58.

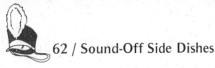

MACARONI FIESTA

1 3/4 c. macaroni
1/2 c. minced green pepper
3 tbsp. butter
2 tbsp. flour
2 c. milk
1 tsp. salt
1/4 tsp. pepper
1/2 tsp. dry mustard
2 c. grated cheese
1/2 c. sliced stuffed olives
2 c. corn flakes

Cook macaroni according to package directions; drain. Cook green pepper in 2 tablespoons butter until soft; stir in flour. Add milk gradually; cook, stirring, until thickened. Add seasonings and 1 cup cheese. Fold in olives; add macaroni. Pour into baking dish. Melt remaining butter; toss corn flakes with butter. Sprinkle over macaroni; top with remaining cheese. Bake in preheated 350-degree oven for 20 minutes or until heated through. Yield: 12 servings.

BAKED NOODLES PAPRIKA

1/2 lb. wide egg noodles
2 tbsp. butter or margarine
2 tbsp. flour
1 c. sour cream
1 c. dry sherry
1 c. cottage cheese
1 tsp. Worcestershire sauce
1 tsp. paprika
Dash of garlic powder
Salt and pepper to taste
2 tbsp. grated Parmesan cheese

Cook noodles in boiling water until tender; drain. Melt butter; stir in flour. Add sour cream and sherry; bring to a boil, stirring constantly. Remove from heat; add cottage cheese, Worcestershire sauce, paprika, garlic powder, salt and pepper. Combine with noodles; turn into greased baking dish. Sprinkle with Parmesan cheese. Bake in preheated 350-degree oven for 40 minutes. Yield: 6 servings.

GERMAN NOODLE CASSEROLE

1 lg. package noodles
1 1-lb. carton cottage cheese
3 c. sour cream
Salt and pepper to taste
Butter
Milk

Cook noodles according to package directions; drain. Arrange layers of noodles, cottage cheese and sour cream in baking dish. Season each layer with salt and pepper; dot with butter. Pour enough milk over mixture in baking dish to moisten well. Bake in preheated 350-degree oven for 45 minutes or until milk is absorbed. Yield: 6-8 servings.

YANKEE DOODLE NOODLE RING

2 c. cooked fine noodles
1 c. grated Cheddar cheese
1 c. bread cubes
2 tbsp. chopped parsley
1 sm. can pimentos, chopped
1 med. onion, chopped
1/2 c. cream
1/4 c. melted butter

Combine all ingredients; mix well. Spoon into buttered ring mold; place mold in pan of water. Bake in preheated 325-degree oven for 40 to 45 minutes. Serve with creamed crab, chicken or ham. Yield: 6 servings.

BATON TWIRLER'S SPAGHETTI AND CHEESE

1 8-oz. wedge mellow cheese
1 8-oz. package spaghetti
1 16-oz. can tomatoes, chopped
Seasonings to taste

Shred cheese. Cook spaghetti according to package directions; drain well. Layer half the spaghetti, half the tomatoes and half the cheese in ungreased 1-quart casserole. Sprinkle with desired seasonings. Repeat layers. Bake in preheated 350-degree oven for 20 minutes. Yield: 6 servings.

FIRST DOWN CHESTNUT DRESSING

1 c. yellow cornmeal
1 c. buttermilk
1 egg
2 tsp. baking powder

1 tsp. soda
Salt
1 tbsp. sugar
10 slices bread
15 crackers
6 hard-cooked eggs, chopped
5 c. broth
1 5-oz. can water chestnuts, chopped
1 tsp. rubbed sage
Pepper to taste

Combine cornmeal, buttermilk, egg, baking powder, soda, 1 teaspoon salt and sugar; mix well. Pour into well-greased pan. Bake in preheated 450-degree oven until done. Brown bread slices and crackers in oven. Crumble corn bread, bread slices and crackers into large bowl; add eggs, broth, water chestnuts and seasonings. Place in greased pan. Bake in preheated 400-degree oven for 20 minutes. Yield: 12 servings.

FRIED PINEAPPLE RINGS

1 tsp. sugar
1/4 c. flour
1 egg, lightly beaten
1/4 tsp. salt
2 tbsp. milk
6 slices pineapple, drained
1/2 c. bread crumbs

Combine sugar and flour. Combine egg, salt and milk. Dredge pineapple with flour mixture; dip in egg mixture. Cover with crumbs. Brown in small amount of hot fat.

ORANGE-CRANBERRY RELISH

2 oranges
4 c. fresh cranberries
2 c. sugar

Cut oranges in quarters; remove seeds but do not peel. Grind oranges and cranberries together; stir in sugar. Place in serving bowl; refrigerate for several hours before serving.

CORN RELISH RECITAL

1/4 c. chopped prepared chutney, drained
1/2 c. sweet pickle relish
1/4 tsp. mustard seed
1 12-oz. can whole kernel corn, drained
1/4 tsp. salt
1 4-oz. jar pimentos, chopped

Combine all ingredients; mix well. Cover; refrigerate. Yield: 6 servings.

CURRIED FRUITS

1 No. 2 can peach halves
1 No. 2 can sliced pineapple
1 No. 2 can pear halves
1/2 c. butter or margarine
3/4 c. (packed) brown sugar
1 tbsp. cornstarch
1 tsp. curry powder

Drain fruits; place in greased casserole. Melt butter; blend in sugar, cornstarch and curry powder. Spoon curry mixture over fruits. Bake in preheated 325-degree oven for 45 minutes. Yield: 8 servings.

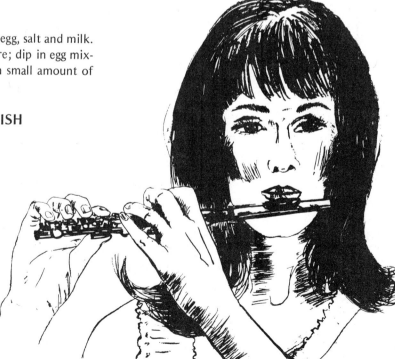

B-Natural Breads

Bread, well known as the staff of life, can be like the steadiest rhythm or the sprightliest melody and still never fail to please. Encompassing airy biscuits and muffins, rich, crusty loaves and rolls, and a host of coffee cakes, pancakes and waffles, bread complements and completes a meal like no other food can. Moreover, home baking is one of the oldest and most pleasurable arts there is to enjoy — for the whole family.

If the sponge rubber texture of commercially prepared breads has caused you and your family to lose interest in breads, then start home baking right away. Not only will you love the results, you will save money too! Prepare *First Chair White Bread* two or three times — you will soon find that your family as well as your guests will settle for nothing less. For a little more variety in your baking repertoire, try *Banana Bread Bossanova* or *Pinwheel Praline Rolls.*

From *Woodwind Waffles* in the morning to *High Note Hush Puppies* and *Cadence Corn Bread* served with an evening fish fry, the band members and cheerleaders feel sure they have offered a bread for every taste and every occasion. These breads you start serving your family may become one of your greatest hits!

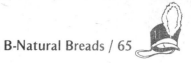

EASY BISCUITS

2 c. sifted flour
3 tsp. baking powder
1 tsp. salt
1 tsp. sugar (opt.)
1/4 c. shortening
2/3 to 3/4 c. milk

Combine flour, baking powder, salt and sugar in bowl; cut in shortening until consistency of cornmeal. Add just enough milk to combine ingredients; mix until combined. Roll out on lightly floured surface; cut with biscuit cutter. Place on cookie sheet. Bake in preheated 425-degree oven for 12 to 15 minutes or until brown. Cheese biscuits may be made by adding 1/2 to 3/4 cup grated cheese to shortening mixture before adding milk. Yield: About 10 medium biscuits.

CHEESE PINWHEELS

3 c. biscuit mix
3/4 c. grated cheese

Prepare biscuit mix according to package directions; knead on floured board for 1 minute. Roll out into thin rectangle; sprinkle with cheese. Roll as for jelly roll; cut into 1/4-inch thick slices. Place on greased baking sheet. Bake in preheated 400-degree oven until brown.

BONGO BISCUITS

2 c. self-rising flour
1 c. milk
1/4 c. mayonnaise

Combine all ingredients in bowl; stir until mixed. Spoon into greased muffin cups. Bake in preheated 400-degree oven for 12 to 15 minutes or until brown. Yield: 10 biscuits.

MAKE-AHEAD BISCUITS

Instant nonfat dry milk
2 c. shortening
2 c. sugar
6 pkg. yeast
Flour
2 tsp. salt

2 tsp. soda
4 tbsp. baking powder

Prepare 2 quarts milk according to dry milk package directions. Pour into saucepan; heat until scalded. Add shortening and sugar; stir until dissolved. Cool to lukewarm. Add yeast; stir until dissolved. Combine enough flour with milk mixture until consistency of pancake batter; let rise for 2 hours. Stir in salt, soda, baking powder and enough flour to make soft, not sticky, dough; mix well. Roll out on floured surface to 1/2-inch thickness; cut with round 3-inch cutter. Place on greased cookie sheet; freeze immediately. Transfer to plastic bags; seal. Store in freezer until ready to bake. Place desired number of biscuits on greased baking sheet. Bake in preheated 450-degree oven until brown. May bake right from freezer or let stand for 10 to 15 minutes before baking. Will keep in freezer for 6 to 8 weeks.

BRAVURA BISCUITS

1/4 c. butter or margarine
2 tbsp. dried celery flakes
2 tbsp. dried onion flakes
1/4 c. grated Parmesan cheese
1 10-count pkg. refrigerator biscuits

Melt butter in pie pan; sprinkle celery and onion flakes over butter. Sprinkle cheese over butter mixture. Separate biscuits; place in pie pan over butter mixture. Bake in preheated 425-degree oven for 10 to 12 minutes or until brown. Invert onto plate; serve. Biscuits may be cut into quarters before baking, if desired.

CRACKLIN' CORN BREAD

2 tbsp. flour
1 1/2 c. cornmeal
2 tsp. sugar
1/2 tsp. salt
3 tsp. baking powder
1 egg, well beaten
1 1/4 c. milk
1 1/2 c. cracklings

Mix flour, cornmeal, sugar, salt and baking powder in bowl. Add egg, milk and cracklings; mix well. Pour into well-greased, deep 9-inch square baking pan. Bake in preheated 425-degree oven for about 20 minutes or until done.

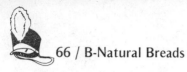

CADENCE CORN BREAD

1 c. sifted all-purpose flour
1/4 c. sugar
4 tbsp. baking powder
3/4 tsp. salt
1 c. cornmeal
2 eggs
1 c. milk
1/4 c. shortening

Sift flour with sugar, baking powder and salt into bowl; stir in cornmeal. Add eggs, milk and shortening; beat with rotary or electric beater until just mixed. Do not overbeat. Pour into greased 9 x 9 x 2-inch pan. Bake in preheated 425-degree oven for 20 to 25 minutes or until done. Batter may be spooned into greased corn stick pans, filling 2/3 full, and baked in 425-degree oven for 12 to 15 minutes.

MEXICAN CORN BREAD

1 1/2 c. cornmeal
3 tsp. baking powder
1 tsp. salt
2 eggs
2/3 c. salad oil
1 c. buttermilk
3 jalapeno peppers, chopped
1 1-lb. can cream-style corn
1 c. grated Cheddar cheese

Mix all ingredients except cheese in order listed. Pour half the batter into greased deep 9-inch square baking dish; sprinkle with half the cheese. Add remaining batter; cover with remaining cheese. Bake in preheated 350-degree oven for 45 minutes or until done. One can whole green chilies, drained and chopped, may be substituted for jalapeno peppers.

HIGH-NOTE HUSH PUPPIES

1 1/2 c. cornmeal
1/2 c. sifted flour
2 tsp. baking powder
1 tbsp. sugar
1/2 tsp. salt
1 sm. onion, finely chopped
1 egg, beaten
3/4 c. milk

Sift dry ingredients together into bowl; mix in onion. Add egg and milk; stir until just mixed. Drop from teaspoon, several at a time, into deep, hot fat; cook until golden brown. Drain on absorbent paper; serve hot. Yield: 2 dozen.

OLD-FASHIONED CORN BREAD MUFFINS

1 c. cornmeal
1 c. flour, sifted
1/2 tsp. salt
2 tsp. baking powder
1 egg, well beaten
1/4 c. shortening
1/4 c. sugar
1 c. milk

Mix first 4 ingredients in bowl; add egg. Mix shortening and sugar well; add to cornmeal mixture. Add milk; mix well. Place in greased muffin pans. Bake in preheated 375-degree oven for 25 minutes or until done.

DRUM MAJOR MUFFINS

2 c. flour
3 tsp. baking powder
3 tbsp. sugar
1 tsp. salt
1/4 c. melted shortening or oil
1 1/4 c. milk
1 egg, beaten

Sift flour, baking powder, sugar and salt into bowl. Add shortening, milk and egg; stir just until flour is dampened. Spoon into greased muffin cups, filling 2/3 full. Bake in preheated 400-degree oven for 20 to 25 minutes or until done. Yield: 12 muffins.

UP-BEAT POPOVERS

2 eggs, beaten
1 c. milk
1 tbsp. melted shortening
1 c. sifted all-purpose flour
1/2 tsp. salt

Combine eggs, milk and shortening. Add flour and salt; beat with rotary or electric beater until smooth and free of lumps. Pour into hot, oiled custard cups or iron muffin pans, filling 1/2 full. Bake in preheated 450-degree oven for 10 minutes. Reduce oven temperature to 350 degrees; bake for 30 minutes longer or until done. Serve immediately. One-fourth cup grated sharp Cheddar cheese may be added to batter, if desired.

REAL COOL MUFFIN MIX

2 c. boiling water
2 c. All-Bran
1 1/4 c. butter
2 1/2 c. sugar
4 eggs
1 qt. buttermilk
4 c. Bran Buds
6 c. flour
5 tsp. soda

Pour boiling water over All-Bran; set aside. Cream butter and sugar in bowl. Add eggs, one at a time, beating well after each addition; stir in All-Bran. Combine buttermilk, Bran Buds, flour and soda in large bowl; blend in All-Bran mixture. Place in gallon jar or plastic bowls; cover. Will keep in refrigerator for several weeks. Bake as many muffins as needed. Spoon batter into greased muffin cups, filling 1/2 full. Bake in preheated 400-degree oven for 10 to 15 minutes or until done.

ORANGE MUFFINS

1 c. sugar
1 c. margarine
1 c. white corn syrup
1/2 c. milk
4 eggs, beaten
1 6-oz. can frozen orange juice, thawed
4 c. flour
2 tsp. soda
2 tsp. salt
1/2 c. chopped nuts
1/2 c. chopped dates or raisins

Mix first 6 ingredients in large bowl. Sift flour with soda and salt; stir in nuts and dates. Add to egg mixture; mix well. Pour into large container; cover. Place in refrigerator; will keep for 1 month. Bake as many muffins as needed. Spoon batter into fluted paper cups in muffin tins, filling 2/3 full. Bake in preheated 375-degree oven for 25 to 30 minutes or until done. Yield: About 3 dozen.

BUTTERHORN ROLLS

1 pkg. yeast
1/2 c. sugar
1/2 c. shortening
1 tsp. salt
2 eggs, well beaten
4 c. sifted flour
Melted butter

Dissolve yeast in 3 tablespoons warm water. Combine sugar, shortening, 1 cup warm water, salt and eggs in large bowl; mix well. Add yeast and flour; beat until smooth. Cover; refrigerate overnight. Roll dough into circle; brush with butter. Cut into 16 triangles. Roll triangles up, beginning with wide end; place on greased baking sheet, point side down. Let rise until doubled in bulk. Bake in preheated 350-degree oven until brown.

DRUM ROLLS

2 c. buttermilk
1 cake or pkg. yeast
1/4 tsp. soda
2 tsp. salt
1/4 c. sugar
4 c. all-purpose flour
2 tbsp. melted margarine

Heat buttermilk until lukewarm. Dissolve yeast in 1/3 cup buttermilk; stir into remaining buttermilk. Add soda, salt and sugar; beat well. Stir in 1/2 of the flour gradually. Combine margarine with yeast mixture; stir in remaining flour gradually. Place in greased bowl; turn dough to grease top. Cover with moist cloth; let rise until doubled in bulk. Shape into rolls; place in greased baking pan. Let rise until doubled in bulk. Bake in preheated 425-degree oven for 15 to 20 minutes or until well browned. Yield: About 24 rolls.

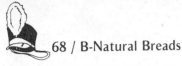

REFRIGERATOR ROLLS

1 qt. milk
1 c. sugar
1 c. mashed potatoes
1 c. melted shortening
12 c. flour
1 tsp. salt
2 tsp. baking powder
1 tsp. soda
2 pkg. yeast

Scald milk; cool to lukewarm. Combine sugar and potatoes in large mixing bowl; mix well. Stir in milk and shortening. Sift 6 cups flour, salt, baking powder and soda together; stir in yeast. Add to potato mixture gradually, mixing well after each addition. Cover dough; let rise for 2 hours. Punch down; work in remaining flour. Cover; refrigerate overnight. Shape dough into rolls; place in greased baking pans. Let rise until almost doubled in bulk. Bake in preheated 400-degree oven for about 15 minutes or until brown. Dough may be kept in refrigerator for 3 days.

PHILADELPHIA STICKY BUNS

3/4 c. milk
1/3 c. sugar
1 tsp. salt
10 tbsp. butter
2 pkg. dry yeast
1 egg, slightly beaten
4 c. (about) flour
1 1/2 c. (packed) dark brown sugar
1/2 c. currants, plumped
1/2 c. chopped pecans
1 tbsp. cinnamon
1 c. dark corn syrup

Scald milk. Stir in sugar, salt and 4 tablespoons butter; cool to lukewarm. Dissolve yeast in 1/3 cup warm water in large bowl. Stir in milk mixture, egg and half the flour; beat until smooth. Stir in enough remaining flour to make soft dough. Turn onto lightly floured board; knead for about 8 minutes or until smooth and elastic, adding flour as needed. Place in greased bowl; turn to grease top. Cover; let rise in warm place for about 1 hour or until doubled in bulk. Mix 1/2 cup brown sugar with currants, pecans and cinnamon; set aside. Mix remaining 1 cup brown sugar, 4 tablespoons butter and corn syrup in saucepan; bring to a boil. Pour into two 9-inch square pans; cool. Punch dough down; divide in half. Roll each half out on floured board to 9 x 14-inch rectangle; spread with remaining 2 tablespoons butter. Sprinkle each rectangle with half the pecan mixture. Roll as for jelly roll from 9-inch side; seal edges. Cut into 1-inch slices; place, cut sides down, in syrup mixture in pans. Cover; let rise in warm place for about 45 minutes or until doubled in bulk. Bake in preheated 350-degree oven for about 25 minutes or until light brown. Invert onto plate; cool. Yield: 18 buns.

HONEY GRAHAM BREAD

2 c. milk, scalded
1/3 c. honey
1 tbsp. salt
1/4 c. Fleischmann's margarine
1/2 c. warm water
2 pkg. or cakes Fleischmann's yeast
2 1/2 c. unsifted graham flour
3 3/4 c. (about) unsifted white flour

Combine milk, honey, salt and margarine; let cool to lukewarm. Measure warm water into large warm bowl; sprinkle in yeast. Add lukewarm milk mixture, graham flour and 2 cups white flour; beat until smooth. Stir in enough additional white flour to make a soft dough. Turn out onto lightly floured board; knead for 8 to 10 minutes or until smooth and elastic. Place in greased bowl; turn to grease top. Cover; let rise in warm place, free from draft, for about 1 hour or until doubled in bulk. Punch down; let rise again for 30 minutes or until doubled in bulk. Punch dough down; turn out onto lightly floured board. Divide in half; shape each half into loaf. Place in 2 greased 9 x 5 x 3-inch loaf pans. Cover; let rise in warm place, free from draft, for 30 minutes until doubled in bulk. Bake in preheated 350-degree oven for 45 minutes or until done. Each half of dough may be formed into a 12-inch roll to make pan rolls. Cut each roll into 12 equal pieces; shape each piece into a smooth ball. Place in 2 greased 9-inch round cake pans. Cover; let rise in warm place, free from draft, for about 30 minutes or until doubled in bulk. Bake in preheated 400-degree oven for about 20 minutes or until done.

Photograph for this recipe on page 64.

Recipes on pages 20 and 24.

PINWHEEL PRALINE ROLLS

1/3 c. scalded milk
1 pkg. yeast
2 1/4 c. sifted flour
2 tbsp. sugar
2 tsp. baking powder
1/2 tsp. salt
2/3 c. butter
1 egg
3/4 c. (packed) brown sugar
1/2 c. chopped nuts

Cool milk to lukewarm. Dissolve yeast in 1/4 cup warm water. Sift flour, sugar, baking powder and salt together into mixing bowl; cut in 1/3 cup butter until mixture resembles fine crumbs. Stir in milk, egg and yeast; beat well. May be stored in refrigerator overnight. Punch dough down. Knead on well-floured surface for 8 to 10 minutes; roll out to 15 x 10-inch rectangle. Cream remaining 1/3 cup butter and brown sugar until fluffy; spread half the mixture over dough. Sprinkle nuts over sugar mixture; roll as for jelly roll from 10-inch side. Cut into 1-inch slices; place on greased cookie sheets. Spread with remaining sugar mixture; let rise in warm place until doubled in bulk. Bake in preheated 425-degree oven for 12 minutes or until done. Yield: 10 rolls.

BUGLE CALL CINNAMON ROLLS

2 pkg. dry yeast
4 c. flour
1/2 c. sugar
1 1/2 tsp. salt
1 egg
1/3 c. oil
1/4 c. melted margarine
1 tsp. cinnamon

Pour 1 1/2 cups warm water into large mixing bowl. Sprinkle yeast over water; let stand for 5 minutes without stirring. Add 2 cups flour, 1/4 cup sugar, salt, egg and oil; beat with mixer until smooth. Stir in remaining 2 cups flour with spoon; beat until smooth. Cover; let rise in warm place until doubled in bulk. Punch down; roll out on floured surface to 1/2-inch thick rectangle. Brush margarine over dough; sprinkle with remaining 1/4 cup sugar and cinnamon. Roll as for jelly roll; cut with sharp knife into desired size rolls. Place on greased baking sheet, cut side down; let

Recipes on pages 89 and 91.

rise in warm place until doubled in bulk. Bake in preheated 375-degree oven for 25 minutes or until brown.

SCOTCH SHORTBREAD FLINGS

1 c. butter
1/2 c. sifted sugar
3 c. sifted flour

Cream butter until light and fluffy; beat in sugar, small amount at a time. Stir in flour, 2 tablespoons at a time; stir until mixture clears side of bowl. Pat firmly into two 8 or 9-inch square pans; prick entire surface with fork. Bake in preheated 300-degree oven for 1 hour or until lightly browned. Cut into squares while warm.

FRENCH BREAD FORTISSIMO

2 pkg. yeast
1 tbsp. salt
1 tbsp. melted margarine
7 c. unsifted flour
Shortening
White cornmeal
1 egg white

Measure 2 1/2 cups warm water into large warm mixing bowl. Sprinkle in yeast; stir until dissolved. Stir in salt and margarine to mix well. Add half the flour; stir until moistened. Add remaining flour; stir until well blended. Finish mixing in flour, using hand if desired; dough will be sticky. Place in well-greased large bowl; turn to grease top. Cover; let stand in warm place for 1 hour and 30 minutes or until doubled in bulk. Measure foil to fit 2 baking sheets. Grease foil with shortening; sprinkle evenly with cornmeal. Shake off excess cornmeal; place foil on baking sheets. Turn out dough on floured board; divide into 4 equal portions. Pat out each portion into 12 x 8-inch oblong. Roll up tightly, beginning at wide side; taper ends gently and seal edges by pressing together. Place loaves on prepared baking sheets. Cover; let stand in warm place for about 1 hour or until doubled in bulk. Make 4 or 5 diagonal cuts on top of each loaf, using razor. Bake in preheated 425-degree oven for 20 minutes. Beat egg white and 1 tablespoon cold water until frothy; brush loaves with egg white mixture. Return to oven; bake for 5 minutes longer. Cool loaves on wire rack.

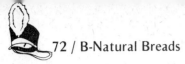

FIRST-CHAIR WHITE BREAD

    2 c. scalded milk
    6 tbsp. sugar
    1/3 c. margarine
    6 tsp. salt
    2 pkg. dry yeast
    9 to 11 c. flour

Mix milk, sugar, margarine and salt thoroughly; stir in 2 cups cold water. Sprinkle yeast over top; stir until dissolved. Add 4 cups flour; beat well with electric mixer. Add enough remaining flour to make soft dough; stir with spoon until mixed. Turn out onto floured board; knead for 8 to 10 minutes. Place in greased bowl; let rise until doubled in bulk. Punch down; let rise again until doubled in bulk. Shape into 4 loaves; place in greased loaf pans. Let rise until doubled in bulk. Bake in preheated 375-degree oven for 30 to 45 minutes or until golden brown. Two cups grated cheese may be added to dough for cheese bread.

COFFEE CAN WHEAT BREAD

    2 c. all-purpose flour
    1 pkg. dry yeast
    1/2 c. milk
    1/2 c. butter
    1/4 c. sugar
    1 tsp. salt
    1/2 c. chopped nuts
    1 c. chopped raisins
    2 c. whole wheat flour
    2 eggs, lightly beaten

Combine all-purpose flour with yeast. Combine 1/2 cup water, milk, butter, sugar and salt in saucepan; place over low heat until butter melts. Cool for about 5 minutes; pour into mixing bowl. Add flour mixture; mix well. Add nuts, raisins, whole wheat flour and eggs; mix well. Dough will be stiff. Turn out onto floured board; knead until smooth and elastic. Grease inside of two 1-pound coffee cans. Divide dough in half; place half the dough in each can. Cover cans with plastic tops; let rise in warm place until dough reaches about 1 inch from tops. Remove plastic tops. Bake in preheated 375-degree oven for 35 minutes or until bread sounds hollow when tapped.

SALT-RISING BREAD

    1 med. potato
    Sugar
    Salt
    2 tbsp. cornmeal
    1 qt. boiling water
    1 c. scalded milk
    Flour
    1 pt. warm water
    1/2 c. shortening

Peel potato; cut into thin slices. Add 1 tablespoon sugar, 1 tablespoon salt and cornmeal to boiling water in saucepan. Stir in potato slices; let stand in warm place overnight or until fermented. Remove potato slices. Pour scalded milk into potato water. Stir in enough flour to make soft dough; beat well. Let stand in warm place until light. Add warm water, 1/2 cup sugar, shortening, 1 teaspoon salt and enough flour to make workable dough; knead on floured surface for about 10 minutes. Shape into loaves; place in greased loaf pans. Let rise until almost doubled in bulk. Bake in preheated 350-degree oven for about 45 minutes or until golden brown.

SWEDISH RYE BREAD

    2 pkg. dry yeast
    1/2 c. warm water
    2 c. sifted rye flour
    3/4 c. dark molasses
    1/3 c. shortening
    2 tsp. salt
    2 c. boiling water
    6 to 6 1/2 c. sifted all-purpose flour
    1 egg, slightly beaten

Dissolve yeast in warm water. Combine rye flour, molasses, shortening and salt in large bowl. Pour in boiling water; blend well. Cool to lukewarm. Add yeast; mix well. Stir in enough all-purpose flour to make soft dough. Turn out onto well-floured surface. Cover; let rest for 10 minutes. Knead for about 10 minutes or until smooth and satiny. Place in lightly greased bowl, turning to grease surface; cover. Let rise in warm place for 1 hour and 30 minutes to 2 hours or until doubled in bulk. Punch down; cover. Let rise for about 30 minutes longer or until almost doubled in bulk. Turn out onto lightly floured surface; divide into 3 equal parts. Shape into balls; cover. Let rest for

15 minutes. Form into round loaves; place on greased baking sheets. Cover; let rise for about 1 hour or until almost doubled in bulk. Brush loaves with egg. Bake in preheated 350-degree oven for 35 to 40 minutes or until bread sounds hollow when tapped.

APRICOT BREAD

1 can apricot nectar
1 1/2 c. chopped dates
1/3 c. dried chopped apricots
1 tbsp. grated orange rind
2 3/4 c. flour
2 tsp. soda
1 tsp. salt
1 tbsp. shortening
1 c. sugar
1 egg, slightly beaten
1/3 c. cream
1/2 c. chopped nuts

Mix apricot nectar, dates and apricots in saucepan; simmer for 5 minutes. Add orange rind; mix well. Sift flour, soda and salt together into bowl; blend in shortening and sugar. Add date mixture, egg, cream and nuts; mix well. Pour into 4 greased and floured 1-pound 4-ounce cans, filling 2/3 full. Bake in preheated 350-degree oven for 50 minutes to 1 hour or until done. Slide bread out of cans immediately; cool. Cut into thin slices to serve.

BANANA BREAD BOSSANOVA

2 c. packaged biscuit mix
3/4 c. sugar
1/4 tsp. soda
1/4 c. chopped nuts
1 c. mashed ripe bananas
2 eggs
1/2 c. sour cream

Combine all ingredients in bowl; mix well. Pour into greased loaf pan. Bake in preheated 350-degree oven for 45 minutes or until done.

CRAZY QUILT BREAD

1/2 c. sugar
1 egg
1 1/4 c. milk
3 c. packaged biscuit mix

1/2 c. mixed candied fruits
3/4 c. chopped nuts

Mix sugar, egg, milk and biscuit mix in bowl; beat vigorously for 30 seconds. Batter will be lumpy. Stir in fruits and nuts; pour into well-greased 9 x 5 x 3-inch loaf pan. Bake in preheated 350-degree oven for 45 minutes or until toothpick inserted in center comes out clean. Remove from pan; cool on wire rack.

ORANGE-DATE BREAD

1/2 c. margarine
1/4 c. sugar
1/2 c. (packed) light brown sugar
2 eggs, beaten
1 tbsp. grated orange peel
1/2 tsp. vanilla extract
1/2 c. sour milk
1/2 c. orange juice
3 c. sifted flour
2 tsp. baking powder
1/2 tsp. soda
1/2 tsp. salt
1 c. chopped dates
1 c. chopped nuts

Cream margarine with sugars in mixing bowl. Add eggs, orange peel and vanilla; beat until light and fluffy. Add sour milk; beat well. Add orange juice; beat thoroughly. Sift flour, baking powder, soda and salt together. Add to creamed mixture; stir just until blended. Fold in dates and nuts; pour into greased 9 x 5 x 3-inch loaf pan. Bake in preheated 350-degree oven for 1 hour to 1 hour and 10 minutes or until bread tests done. Remove from pan; cool on wire rack.

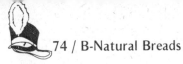

MINCEMEAT BREAD RING

1 3/4 c. all-purpose flour
3 tsp. baking powder
1/2 tsp. salt
2 eggs, well beaten
1/4 c. milk
1/2 c. (packed) brown sugar
3 tbsp. melted butter
1 c. prepared mincemeat
1/4 c. orange marmalade
1/2 c. soft butter

Sift flour, baking powder and salt together. Beat eggs well; stir in milk, brown sugar, melted butter and mincemeat. Add flour mixture; stir until just blended. Place in 8-inch greased ring mold. Bake in preheated 350-degree oven for 1 hour or until done; cool for 10 minutes. Remove from mold; mix orange marmalade and butter. Serve bread with orange butter. Yield: 12 slices.

FRESH APPLE COFFEE CAKE

1 egg, beaten
1/2 c. milk
1/4 c. vegetable oil
1 c. grated tart apples
1 1/2 c. flour
1/2 c. sugar
2 tsp. baking powder
1/2 tsp. salt
1 tsp. cinnamon
1/3 c. (packed) brown sugar
1/3 c. chopped pecans

Combine egg, milk, oil and apples in bowl; mix well. Add flour, sugar, baking powder, salt and 1/2 tea-spoon cinnamon; stir until just mixed. Place in greased 9-inch square baking pan. Combine brown sugar, pecans and remaining 1/2 teaspoon cinnamon; sprinkle over batter. Bake in preheated 375-degree oven for about 35 minutes or until done. Yield: 9 servings.

BLUEBERRY COFFEE CAKE

1 1/4 c. sugar
1/4 c. butter
1 egg

2 1/3 c. flour
2 tsp. baking powder
1 tsp. salt
1/2 c. milk
2 1/2 c. drained blueberries
3 tbsp. soft butter

Combine 3/4 cup sugar, butter and egg in mixing bowl; mix well. Sift 2 cups flour, baking powder and 1/2 teaspoon salt together; add to sugar mixture alternately with milk, beating well after each addition. Stir in blueberries. Place in greased 8 x 10-inch baking pan. Combine remaining 1/2 cup sugar, 1/3 cup flour and 1/2 teaspoon salt with soft butter; sprinkle over batter. Bake in preheated 375-degree oven for about 25 minutes or until done.

CINNAMON-SOUR CREAM COFFEE CAKE

1/2 c. butter or margarine
Sugar
2 eggs
1 1/3 c. sour cream
1 1/2 tsp. vanilla extract
1 1/2 c. flour
1/4 tsp. salt
1 tsp. baking powder
1 tsp. soda
2 tsp. cinnamon
1/4 c. grated orange peel
3/4 c. chopped nuts

Cream butter and 1 cup sugar in bowl. Add eggs; beat well. Mix sour cream and vanilla. Sift flour, salt, bak-ing powder and soda together; add to creamed mix-ture alternately with sour cream mixture. Mix 1/3 cup sugar, cinnamon and orange peel. Pour half the batter into well-greased and floured tube pan; sprinkle with half the cinnamon mixture. Add re-maining batter; swirl through batter with knife. Add remaining cinnamon mixture; sprinkle with nuts. Bake in preheated 350-degree oven for 45 minutes or until done.

MIDMORNING COFFEE CAKE

1/2 c. shortening
3/4 c. sugar

1 tsp. vanilla extract
3 eggs
2 c. flour
1 tsp. baking powder
1 tsp. soda
1/2 pt. sour cream
1/2 c. butter
1 c. (packed) brown sugar
2 tsp. cinnamon
1 c. chopped walnuts

Cream shortening with sugar and vanilla in bowl. Add eggs, one at a time, beating well after each addition. Sift flour, baking powder and soda together; add to creamed mixture alternately with sour cream. Mix butter, brown sugar, cinnamon and walnuts in bowl. Pour half the batter into greased tube pan; add half the brown sugar mixture. Repeat layers. Bake in pre-heated 350-degree oven for 50 minutes or until done; cool. Drizzle with confectioners' sugar icing, if desired.

TIME-OUT LEMON COFFEE CAKE

4 c. packaged biscuit mix
3/4 c. (packed) brown sugar
1 tsp. cinnamon
1/4 tsp. nutmeg
1 1/4 c. milk
1 egg, beaten
6 tbsp. melted butter
1 tsp. grated lemon peel
1/4 c. chopped walnuts

Combine biscuit mix, 1/4 cup brown sugar and spices in bowl; mix well. Combine milk, egg and 4 table-spoons butter. Add to dry ingredients; beat for 30 seconds. Mix remaining 1/2 cup brown sugar, lemon peel and walnuts. Pour half the batter into greased 9 x 9-inch baking pan. Drizzle with 1 tablespoon re-maining butter; sprinkle with half the walnut mix-ture. Repeat layers. Bake in preheated 350-degree oven for about 35 minutes or until done; serve warm.

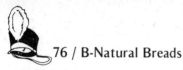

SUGARPLUM RING

1 pkg. yeast
1/2 c. scalded milk
Sugar
1/3 c. shortening
1 tsp. salt
4 c. sifted flour
2 eggs, beaten
1/4 c. melted butter
1 tsp. cinnamon
1/2 c. whole blanched almonds
1/2 c. whole candied red cherries
1/2 c. dark corn syrup

Dissolve yeast in 1/4 cup warm water. Combine milk, 1/3 cup sugar, shortening and salt in large bowl; cool to lukewarm. Stir in 1 cup flour; beat well. Add yeast and eggs; mix well. Add enough remaining flour to make soft dough; mix thoroughly. Place in greased bowl; turn to grease surface. Cover; let rise for 2 hours or until doubled in bulk. Punch down; let stand for 10 minutes. Divide dough into 4 parts. Cut each part into 10 pieces; shape into balls. Roll balls in butter. Combine 3/4 cup sugar and cinnamon; roll balls in cinnamon mixture. Arrange 1/3 of the balls in greased 10-inch tube pan. Sprinkle 1/3 of the almonds and cherries over balls. Repeat layers twice. Mix corn syrup with remaining butter and cinnamon mixture; drizzle over top. Cover; let rise in warm place for 1 hour or until doubled in bulk. Bake in preheated 350-degree oven for 35 minutes or until done. Cool for 5 minutes; invert onto large platter.

SPICY DUNKING DOUGHNUTS

4 eggs
Sugar
1/3 c. milk
1/3 c. melted shortening
3 1/2 c. sifted flour
3 tsp. baking powder
3/4 tsp. salt
2 tsp. cinnamon
1/2 tsp. nutmeg

Place eggs and 2/3 cup sugar in bowl; beat until well mixed. Add milk and shortening; mix well. Sift flour, baking powder, salt, 1 teaspoon cinnamon, and nutmeg together. Add to egg mixture; mix well. Chill thoroughly. Roll out 3/8 inch thick on lightly floured surface; cut with floured doughnut cutter. Let stand for 15 minutes. Fry in deep fat at 375 degrees until brown, turning once; drain on paper towels. Place 1/2 cup sugar and remaining 1 teaspoon cinnamon in bag. Add doughnuts; shake until coated. Yield: About 2 dozen.

QUICK DOUGHNUTS

1 pt. salad oil
1 pkg. refrigerator biscuits
1/2 c. sugar
1 tsp. cinnamon

Heat oil in skillet. Separate biscuits; cut hole in center of each with empty soft drink bottle top. Cook biscuits and holes in hot oil for 3 to 5 minutes or until golden brown. Place sugar and cinnamon in paper sack; shake doughnuts and holes in sack until coated.

GLAZED YEAST DOUGHNUTS

2 pkg. dry yeast
1/2 c. warm water
1 c. boiling water
1/4 c. shortening
3/4 c. sugar
1 1/3 c. milk
2 lg. eggs, well beaten
7 1/2 c. flour
1 tsp. nutmeg (opt.)
Salad oil or shortening
3 c. confectioners' sugar
1 tsp. vanilla extract

Dissolve yeast in warm water. Combine boiling water, shortening and sugar in large bowl; stir in 1 cup milk. Add eggs and yeast; mix well. Add flour and nutmeg; mix until smooth. Place in greased bowl; cover. Chill for 2 to 3 hours or overnight. Divide in half; roll out on floured board to 1/2-inch thickness. Cut with 3-inch doughnut cutter; let rise in warm place until doubled in bulk. Fry in deep oil at 375 degrees until lightly browned; drain on absorbent paper. Combine confectioners' sugar, remaining 1/3 cup milk and vanilla; beat until smooth. Spread over doughnuts while warm. May coat doughnuts with confectioners' sugar or sugar instead of glaze, if desired. Yield: 4 1/2 dozen.

TRIPLE-TIME PANCAKES

2 c. sifted flour
3 tsp. baking powder
1/4 c. sugar
1 tsp. salt
2 eggs, well beaten
2 c. milk
1/3 c. salad oil

Sift flour with baking powder, sugar and salt. Mix eggs, milk and oil in bowl. Add dry ingredients; beat until mixed. Drop by tablespoonfuls onto hot griddle. Cook until underside is golden brown and bubbles appear over surface. Turn; cook until underside is golden brown.

BUTTERMILK PANCAKES

2 c. sifted flour
1 tsp. soda
1 tsp. salt
2 tbsp. sugar
2 eggs, slightly beaten
2 c. buttermilk
2 tbsp. melted butter

Sift flour, soda, salt and sugar into bowl. Add eggs, buttermilk and butter; stir until just mixed. Mixture will be lumpy. Pour 1/4 cup batter for each pancake onto hot, greased griddle; cook until bubbles cover surface. Turn; brown on other side. Serve with butter and syrup.

BLUEBERRY PANCAKES

1 c. sifted flour
1 1/2 tsp. baking powder
1 tbsp. sugar
1/2 tsp. salt
1/4 tsp. cinnamon
1 egg, separated
2 tbsp. melted butter
3/4 c. milk
3/4 c. drained blueberries

Sift flour with baking powder, sugar, salt and cinnamon into bowl. Beat egg yolk until thick and lemon colored; beat egg white until stiff peaks form. Add butter to egg yolk; stir in milk. Add to dry ingredients; stir until just mixed. Fold in egg white; fold in blueberries. Drop by spoonfuls onto hot griddle; cook until lightly browned on both sides. Serve with butter.

CHOCOLATE WAFFLES

2 c. flour
3 tsp. baking powder
1/2 tsp. salt
3 tbsp. cocoa
1/4 c. sugar
2 eggs, separated
1/4 c. melted butter
1 1/4 c. milk
1 tsp. vanilla extract

Sift first 5 ingredients together into large mixing bowl; stir in well-beaten egg yolks, butter, milk and vanilla. Beat egg whites until stiff peaks form; fold into flour mixture. Fill bottom of hot waffle iron with batter; close top. Bake until brown. Repeat with remaining batter. May be served with ice cream, if desired.

WOODWIND WAFFLES

2 c. all-purpose flour
3 tsp. baking powder
3/4 tsp. salt
2 tbsp. sugar
3 eggs, separated
1 3/4 c. milk
1/2 c. salad oil

Sift flour with baking powder, salt and sugar 3 times; place in bowl. Beat egg yolks; stir in milk and oil. Pour into flour mixture; beat until smooth. Fold in stiffly beaten egg whites. Pour 1/2 cup batter for each waffle into hot waffle iron; bake until golden brown. Serve with butter and syrup or honey.

Do-Re-Mi Desserts

If you asked a group of children, teenagers and adults to name just a few of their favorite foods, cakes, cookies and pies are sure to be the most frequent answers. Because desserts are so popular, it is no wonder that the band members and cheerleaders thought this section should be the biggest and best of all.

And, so it is — simply chocked full of fantastic recipes for some of the most irresistible desserts you've ever tasted. Desserts like *Fabulous Finale, Lemon Lyre Delight* and *Chocolate Cheers* will bring nothing but enthusiastic compliments from both your family and friends. A refreshingly cool combination that the younger generation will really go for is *Take Five Sugar Cookies* and *Schubert's Cranberry Sherbet*.

All year long, boys and girls want to know how they can raise money for new uniforms, a class trip or a new trophy case. Bake sales are the ideal solution. Homemade *Confetti Cookies* and *Rock and Roll Candy* are two sweets that will really sell. Since anytime is the right time for Do-Re-Mi Desserts, why not try one today?

FRESH COCONUT CAKE

1 c. shortening
2 c. sugar
1 tsp. vanilla extract
3 c. sifted cake flour
3 tsp. baking powder
1 tsp. salt
1/2 c. milk
1/2 c. coconut milk
1 c. grated fresh coconut
6 egg whites, stiffly beaten

Grease and flour bottoms of two 9-inch layer cake pans. Cream shortening and sugar until fluffy; stir in vanilla. Combine flour, baking powder and salt; add creamed mixture alternately with milk and coconut milk, beating well after each addition. Stir in coconut; fold in egg whites carefully but thoroughly. Turn into pans. Bake in preheated 375-degree oven for 30 minutes. Cool in pans for 10 minutes. Turn out onto wire rack.

Coconut Icing

Sugar
1/4 c. coconut milk
1/4 tsp. salt
1/2 tsp. cream of tartar
2 egg whites
1 tsp. vanilla extract
2 c. grated fresh coconut

Add 1 teaspoon sugar to coconut milk; spoon over cake layers. Combine 1 cup sugar, salt, cream of tartar, egg whites, 3 tablespoons water and vanilla in top of double boiler. Cook for 7 minutes, beating constantly with mixer at high speed. Stir in 1 1/2 cups coconut. Frost between layers and over cake; sprinkle cake with remaining coconut.

ITALIAN DREAM CAKE

1/2 c. margarine
1/2 c. vegetable shortening
2 c. sugar
5 eggs, separated
2 c. flour
1 tsp. soda
1 c. buttermilk
1 tsp. vanilla extract
1 sm. can flaked coconut
1 c. chopped pecans

Cream margarine and shortening; add sugar, beating until smooth. Add egg yolks; beat well. Combine flour and soda; add to creamed mixture alternately with buttermilk. Stir in vanilla, coconut and pecans. Fold in stiffly beaten egg whites. Pour into 3 greased 9-inch pans. Bake in preheated 350-degree oven for 25 minutes or until done.

Cream Cheese Frosting

1 8-oz. package cream cheese, softened
1/4 c. margarine
1 1-lb. box powdered sugar
1 tsp. vanilla extract
1 c. chopped pecans

Beat cream cheese and margarine until fluffy. Blend in sugar gradually; stir in vanilla. Spread frosting between layers, over top and around side. Sprinkle pecans over top.

PINEAPPLE UPSIDE-DOWN CAKE

1 c. (packed) brown sugar
2 tbsp. butter, melted
1 can sliced pineapple
2 c. sugar
Flour
2 eggs
2 tsp. baking powder
2 c. cream
1 tsp. vanilla extract

Sprinkle brown sugar and butter in bottom of iron skillet or pan. Drain pineapple; reserve juice. Layer pineapple over brown sugar. Mix 1 cup sugar, 2 cups flour, 1 egg, baking powder, 1 cup cream and vanilla thoroughly; pour over pineapple. Bake in preheated 350-degree oven for 20 minutes or until cake tests done. Invert on plate. Combine remaining 1 cup sugar and 2 tablespoons flour; mix well. Heat remaining 1 cup cream and reserved juice in saucepan; stir in sugar mixture until blended. Cook until slightly thickened. Beat remaining egg well; add small amount of cream mixture to egg, stirring constantly. Return egg mixture to saucepan; cook, stirring constantly, until thickened. Serve sauce with cake.

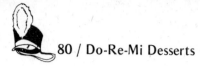

GRAPEFRUIT CAKE

1 1/2 c. sugar
1 tbsp. finely grated grapefruit rind
1/2 tsp. finely grated lemon rind
3/4 c. butter
3 eggs
1/2 c. grapefruit juice
3 c. cake flour
3/4 tsp. salt
3 1/2 tsp. baking powder
1/4 tsp. soda

Place sugar, grated rinds and butter in mixing bowl; cream until light and fluffy. Add eggs, one at a time, beating well after each addition. Combine grapefruit juice and 1/2 cup water; stir juice mixture into egg mixture. Sift cake flour with salt, baking powder and soda; stir into egg mixture, a small amount at a time, mixing lightly after each addition. Pour into 2 greased 9-inch layer cake pans. Bake in preheated 375-degree oven for 30 minutes or until brown. Cool cakes in pans for about 10 minutes; invert onto wire racks. Cool.

Fluffy Grapefruit-Cheese Frosting

3 3-oz. packages cream cheese, softened
1 tbsp. butter, softened
4 tsp. finely grated grapefruit rind
1 tsp. finely grated lemon rind
1 tsp. finely grated orange rind
1/4 tsp. vanilla extract
4 c. confectioners' sugar
Sections from 2 grapefruit and 2 oranges

Place cream cheese, butter, rinds and vanilla in bowl; beat until fluffy. Beat in sugar, small amount at a time, until fluffy and of spreading consistency. Spread thin layer of frosting between layers; frost top and side of cake, swirling frosting. Garnish with alternating grapefruit and orange sections around top of cake and with clusters of fruit at base. Yield: 8 servings.

COCONUT-CHOCOLATE SWIRL CAKE

1 box coconut-pecan frosting mix
1 pkg. German chocolate cake mix
1 tbsp. sugar
1 c. water
1/2 c. oil
4 eggs
1 to 1 1/2 c. chocolate chips

Spray a 10-inch bundt pan with Pam. Combine 1 cup frosting mix, cake mix, sugar, water, oil and eggs; beat until well blended. Pour 1/3 of the batter into prepared pan. Sprinkle 1/2 cup remaining frosting mix over batter; sprinkle half the chocolate chips over the frosting mix. Add half the remaining batter, then 1/2 cup frosting mix. Add remaining chocolate chips. Add remaining batter; sprinkle with remaining frosting mix. Bake in preheated 350-degree oven for 55 to 60 minutes or until cake tests done. Cool in pan for 30 minutes; remove from pan.

Try using a string instead of a knife when a cake is to be cut while it is hot.

SOUTHERN LANE CAKE

3 1/4 c. sifted cake flour
3 1/2 tsp. baking powder
1/2 tsp. salt
1 c. butter or margarine
2 c. sugar
1 tsp. vanilla extract
1 c. milk
8 egg whites, stiffly beaten

Sift flour with baking powder and salt. Cream the butter and sugar until light and fluffy; add vanilla. Add flour mixture alternately with milk, beating well after each addition. Fold in egg whites. Grease bottoms of three 9-inch layer pans; line with waxed paper. Pour batter into layer pans. Bake in preheated 375-degree oven for 25 to 30 minutes. Cool.

Filling

8 egg yolks, lightly beaten
1 1/4 c. sugar
1/2 c. butter or margarine
1 c. chopped pecans
1 c. grated fresh coconut
1 c. chopped candied cherries
1/3 c. whiskey or wine
1 c. chopped seedless raisins

Combine egg yolks, sugar and butter in a saucepan. Cook over low heat for about 5 minutes or until slightly thickened, stirring constantly. Stir in remaining ingredients; cool. Spread between cake layers.

Frosting

    2 1/2 c. sugar
    1/8 tsp. salt
    1/3 c. light corn syrup
    2/3 c. water
    2 egg whites
    1 tsp. vanilla extract

Combine sugar, salt, syrup and water in saucepan; cook over low heat, stirring, until sugar dissolves. Bring to a boil without stirring. Beat egg whites until foamy. Add 3 tablespoons syrup mixture slowly; beat until stiff but not dry. Cook remaining syrup mixture to hard-ball stage or 265 degrees on candy thermometer. Add to egg whites slowly, beating constantly; beat until frosting begins to lose gloss and holds shape. Stir in vanilla; spread over top and side of cake.

ORANGE MOTHER'S DAY CAKE

    1 18 1/2-oz. package spice cake mix
    2 tbsp. grated orange rind
    2/3 c. Florida orange juice
    4 eggs
    1 18 1/2-oz. package yellow cake mix

Prepare spice cake mix according to package directions, adding 1 tablespoon grated orange rind and substituting 1/3 cup orange juice for part of the water. Add 2 eggs as directed; turn batter into 2 greased and floured 9-inch layer cake pans. Bake in preheated 350-degree oven for 25 to 30 minutes or until cake tester inserted in center of cake comes out clean. Cool for 10 minutes; turn out on cake rack to cool completely. Prepare yellow cake mix according to package directions, adding remaining 1 tablespoon grated rind and substituting remaining 1/3 cup orange juice for part of the water. Add remaining 2 eggs as directed. Turn half the batter into 1 greased and floured 9-inch layer cake pan; spoon remaining batter into 12 muffin pan cups lined with paper liners. Bake in preheated 350-degree oven for 25 to 30 minutes for layer and 15 to 20 minutes for cupcakes. Cool layer for 10 minutes; turn out on cake rack to cool completely. Cool cupcakes.

Orange Filling

    1 3 1/4-oz. package vanilla pudding and
      pie filling mix
    1 3/4 c. milk
    1/4 c. Florida frozen orange juice
      concentrate, thawed

Combine pudding mix and milk in medium saucepan. Place over low heat; cook until mixture thickens and comes to a boil, stirring constantly. Remove from heat; stir in undiluted orange juice concentrate. Chill thoroughly. Place one spice cake layer on plate; spread with half the filling. Top with yellow cake layer; spread with remaining filling. Top with remaining spice cake layer.

Frosting and Decoration

    1 7-oz. package fluffy white frosting mix
    1 3 1/2-oz. can flaked coconut
    Decorating frosting tubes
    Florida orange slices

Prepare frosting mix according to package directions. Frost cupcakes and side and top of cake. Coat side of cake with coconut. Write MOM on top of cake with decorating frosting; write children's names on cupcakes. Place halved orange slices around base of cake. Wrap a small dowel with ribbon; insert about 1 inch into center of cake. Attach a ribbon for each child's cupcake to top of dowel; place other end of ribbon under cupcake.

Photograph for this recipe on page 87.

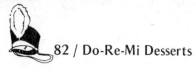

ORANGE SLICE CAKE

1 1/2 c. margarine
2 c. sugar
1 tsp. soda
1/2 c. buttermilk
2 lb. orange slice candy
1   1-lb. package flaked coconut
1   8-oz. package pitted dates, diced
2 c. chopped nuts
3 1/2 c. flour
4 eggs
1   6-oz. can frozen orange juice, thawed
2 c. powdered sugar

Cream margarine and sugar until sugar is dissolved. Dissolve soda in buttermilk. Cut candy in small pieces. Combine candy, coconut, dates and nuts in large bowl. Add enough flour to coat candy mixture. Add buttermilk mixture to creamed mixture alternately with remaining flour. Add eggs, one at a time, beating well after each addition. Fold in candy mixture. Turn into 3 well-greased and floured loaf pans. Batter should be 1 inch from tops of pans. Bake in preheated 250-degree oven for 2 hours and 30 minutes to 3 hours. Combine the orange juice and powdered sugar in saucepan; bring to a boil. Remove cakes from oven; prick tops with fork. Pour syrup on cakes immediately. Let stand in pans overnight to cool.

OLD-FASHIONED GINGERBREAD

2 3/4 c. sifted all-purpose flour
1 tsp. salt
1 tsp. soda
1 tsp. ginger
1 tsp. cinnamon
1/2 c. soft butter
1/2 c. sugar
2 eggs
1 c. molasses
1 c. buttermilk

Sift flour, salt, soda, ginger and cinnamon together into mixing bowl. Cream butter until light and fluffy. Add sugar to butter gradually, beating well after each addition. Add eggs, one at a time, beating well after each addition. Stir in molasses. Add flour mixture alternately with buttermilk; mix until smooth after each addition. Pour into buttered and floured 13 x 9 x 2-inch baking pan. Bake in preheated 350-degree oven for 35 minutes or until gingerbread tests done. Serve topped with slightly sweetened whipped cream and sliced bananas, if desired.

Photograph for this recipe on page 78.

CAKE SQUARES WITH CRANBERRY APRICOT SAUCE

1 pkg. yellow cake mix
1 tsp. ground nutmeg
2 c. Ocean Spray fresh cranberries
1/2 c. sugar
1 c. apricot jam
1   6-oz. can frozen orange juice concentrate
1/2 lemon, sliced thin

Prepare cake mix according to package directions, adding nutmeg to batter. Pour batter into greased and floured 13 x 9 x 2-inch pan. Bake according to package directions. Combine remaining ingredients in saucepan; bring to a boil. Simmer for 10 minutes or until cranberries are tender, stirring occasionally. Cut cake into 1-inch cubes; place in serving dishes. Spoon hot sauce over top of cake cubes. Yield: 12 servings.

Photograph for this recipe on page 28.

CARAMEL CORN CONFECTION

2 c. (packed) brown sugar
1/2 c. dark corn syrup
1 c. margarine
1/2 tsp. cream of tartar
1 tsp. soda
6 qt. popped popcorn

Combine brown sugar, syrup, margarine and cream of tartar in saucepan. Bring to a hard boil, stirring until sugar is melted; boil for 5 minutes. Remove from heat; stir in soda. Pour over popcorn; mix well. Place in roaster. Bake in preheated 250-degree oven for about 1 hour, stirring occasionally. Store in tightly covered containers.

CHOW MEIN CANDY

1 pkg. chocolate bits
1 c. butterscotch bits

1 can chow mein noodles
1 c. chopped cashew nuts

Melt chocolate and butterscotch bits in top of double boiler. Remove from heat; stir in chow mein noodles and cashew nuts. Drop by spoonfuls onto waxed paper. Let cool.

MILLION DOLLAR FUDGE

4 1/2 c. sugar
1/8 tsp. salt
2 tbsp. butter
1 tall can evaporated milk
1 12-oz. package semisweet chocolate bits
2 c. marshmallow creme
2 c. chopped nuts

Combine sugar, salt, butter and milk in saucepan; boil for 6 minutes. Combine remaining ingredients in bowl; stir in milk mixture. Beat until chocolate is melted. Pour into buttered square pan; chill for several hours before cutting.

NEW ORLEANS PECAN PRALINES

1 1/2 c. pecan halves
1 c. (packed) dark brown sugar
1 c. sugar
1/3 stick butter
1/3 c. milk
1 tsp. vanilla extract

Combine pecan halves, sugars and butter in saucepan. Bring milk to a boil; pour over pecan mixture. Place over medium heat; cook for 7 minutes, stirring occasionally. Remove from heat; add vanilla. Beat for about 30 seconds. Drop by tablespoonfuls onto waxed paper.

ROCK AND ROLL CANDY

4 4 1/2-oz. milk chocolate bars
3 c. miniature marshmallows
3/4 c. coarsely broken walnuts

Melt chocolate bars partially over hot water; remove from heat. Beat until smooth. Stir in marshmallows and walnuts. Spread in buttered 8 x 8 x 2-inch pan; chill thoroughly. Cut into squares.

CHOCOLATE CHEERS

2 sq. baking chocolate
1 can sweetened condensed milk
3 c. coconut
1/2 tsp. salt
1 tsp. vanilla extract

Melt chocolate over hot water. Add condensed milk, coconut, salt and vanilla; mix well. Drop by teaspoonfuls onto well-greased cookie sheet. Bake in preheated 250-degree oven until lightly browned. Remove cookies from sheet immediately; place on wire rack to cool. Yield: 3 dozen cookies.

CONFETTI COOKIES

1 c. sugar
1/2 c. (packed) brown sugar
1 c. shortening
2 eggs
1 tsp. vanilla extract
2 1/3 c. all-purpose flour
1 tsp. salt
1 tsp. soda
1 c. small cut-up gumdrops
1/2 c. chopped nuts

Combine sugars, shortening, eggs and vanilla; cream until fluffy. Sift flour, salt and soda together; add to creamed mixture, mixing well. Stir in gumdrops and nuts. Drop by teaspoonfuls onto greased baking sheet. Bake in preheated 350-degree oven for 15 minutes or until browned. Yield: 5-6 dozen.

HELLO DOLLY BARS

1/2 c. butter or margarine
1 c. graham cracker crumbs
1 c. flaked coconut
1 c. semisweet chocolate chips
1 c. chopped nuts
1 can sweetened condensed milk

Melt butter in 9 x 9 x 2-inch pan; sprinkle crumbs over butter. Add coconut, chocolate chips and nuts in layers; pour milk over nuts. Do not stir. Bake in preheated 325-degree oven for 30 minutes. Cool. Cut into bars.

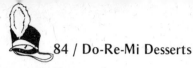

LEMON DELIGHTS

1 box lemon cake mix
1 4 1/2-oz. carton Cool Whip
1 egg
Confectioners' sugar

Combine all ingredients except confectioners' sugar; mix well. Shape into small balls; roll in confectioners' sugar. Place on baking sheet. Bake in preheated 350-degree oven for about 8 minutes or until lightly browned.

TAKE FIVE SUGAR COOKIES

2 c. sugar
4 eggs
1 c. butter, softened
1 tsp. soda
1 tsp. vanilla extract
7 c. (about) flour

Beat sugar and eggs together until light and fluffy. Beat into butter until well mixed. Add soda, vanilla and half the flour; mix well. Work in remaining flour to make a stiff dough. Roll out part of the dough at a time on floured board; cut into desired shapes, using floured cookie cutters. Sprinkle with additional sugar; place on greased baking sheets. Bake in preheated 400-degree oven for 8 to 10 minutes or until lightly browned. Plain cookies may be iced with confectioners' sugar icing, if desired.

PEACHY CREAM PUFFS

1 c. water
3/4 c. butter
1 c. all-purpose flour
1/2 tsp. salt
4 eggs
1/4 c. sugar
1/4 c. cornstarch
2 12-oz. cans apricot nectar
1/3 c. peach brandy
Butter pecan ice cream
Sliced peaches

Bring water and 1/2 cup butter to a rolling boil in 2-quart saucepan. Add flour and salt all at once; stir vigorously over low heat until mixture leaves side of pan and is smooth and satiny. Remove from heat; transfer dough to large mixing bowl. Add eggs, one at a time, beating well after each addition. Drop 3 tablespoons dough for each puff onto buttered baking sheets about 2 inches apart. Bake in preheated 425-degree oven for 20 to 30 minutes or until golden brown. Turn off oven heat. Make a small slit in each puff; return to oven for 20 minutes to dry centers. Cool on wire rack. Cut off tops; remove soft filaments from insides. Combine sugar and cornstarch in saucepan; add apricot nectar. Cook, stirring constantly, until mixture boils. Boil for 2 minutes, stirring constantly. Remove from heat; add remaining 1/4 cup butter. Stir until melted. Pour sauce into chafing dish; keep warm. Stir in brandy. Fill cream puffs with ice cream; place on serving dish. Arrange sliced peaches around cream puffs; spoon sauce over cream puffs. Serve immediately. Yield: 15 servings.

Photograph for this recipe on page 88.

WALNUT BROWNIES

3/4 c. butter
1 1/2 c. sugar
3 eggs, well beaten
3 sq. chocolate, melted
Pinch of salt
3/4 c. flour
Chopped walnuts to taste
1/4 c. powdered sugar

Cream butter and sugar until fluffy. Stir in eggs and chocolate. Add salt, flour and walnuts; mix well. Place in buttered 8-inch square pan. Bake in preheated 350-degree oven for about 40 minutes or until done. Remove from oven; sprinkle with powdered sugar. Cool; cut as desired.

TEMPO LEMON TORTE

1 pkg. lemon pie filling mix
2 egg whites
1 tbsp. sugar
Whipped cream
3/4 c. vanilla wafer crumbs

Prepare pie filling mix according to package directions; let cool. Beat egg whites until frothy. Add sugar gradually; beat until stiff. Fold egg whites and 3/4 cup whipped cream into lemon filling. Spread 1/2 cup crumbs in buttered pan; pour in filling. Sprinkle remaining crumbs over filling. Freeze until firm. Serve with whipped cream; garnish with cherries, if desired. Yield: 6 servings.

LEMON FRUIT PARFAITS

1 tbsp. cornstarch
1/2 c. sugar
Dash of salt
1 1/4 c. milk
1 egg yolk, slightly beaten
2 tbsp. butter
1 tsp. lemon peel
3 tbsp. fresh lemon juice
2 drops of yellow food coloring
Mixed fresh fruits
Vanilla ice cream

Combine cornstarch, sugar and salt in 1-quart saucepan; blend in milk. Bring to a boil, stirring constantly; cook and stir for 2 minutes. Remove from heat. Stir a small amount of hot mixture into egg yolk; stir egg yolk into hot mixture. Cook for 1 minute, stirring constantly. Add butter, lemon peel and lemon juice; stir until butter is melted. Stir in food coloring. Chill thoroughly. Arrange layer of fruits in glass; spoon on lemon sauce. Place ice cream on top of sauce. Repeat layers to fill glass, ending with ice cream.

Photograph for this recipe on page 88.

GRANDMA'S PEACH ICE CREAM

1 1/2 c. milk
1 c. sugar
2 tbsp. flour
Dash of salt
2 eggs
1 1/2 tsp. vanilla extract
1 1/2 c. heavy cream
1 1/2 c. fresh peach puree
Almond extract to taste

Scald milk in top of double boiler. Combine 3/4 cup sugar, flour and salt; stir in enough hot milk to make a smooth paste. Stir paste into hot milk. Cook, stirring, until thickened. Cover; cook for 10 minutes. Beat eggs lightly; stir cooked mixture into eggs, a small amount at a time. Return to double boiler; cook for 1 minute longer, stirring constantly. Let

cool. Stir in all remaining ingredients; pour into 2-quart ice cream freezer container. Pack with ice and salt; freeze according to freezer instructions.

VICTORY VANILLA ICE CREAM

4 c. milk
6 eggs, beaten
3 c. sugar
2 tbsp. flour
1 tall can evaporated milk
1 tsp. vanilla extract

Heat 2 cups milk in saucepan until hot. Combine eggs, sugar, flour and evaporated milk. Add to heated milk; cook, stirring occasionally, until sugar is dissolved. Remove from heat; let cool. Add vanilla and remaining 2 cups milk. Pour into freezer container. Freeze according to freezer instructions. Yield: 1 gallon.

SCHUBERT'S CRANBERRY SHERBET

4 c. cranberries
3 c. sugar
1 tbsp. lemon juice
2 c. milk or 1 c. milk and 1 c. cream
1/2 c. finely chopped black walnuts

Cook cranberries in 2 cups water for 10 minutes or until cranberries pop open. Press through sieve. Combine cranberry juice, sugar and lemon juice; stir in milk. Add walnuts. Place in freezer; freeze until firm, stirring occasionally.

OLD-FASHIONED ICE CREAM

6 eggs
2 c. sugar
2 qt. whipping cream
2 tbsp. vanilla extract
1 qt. (about) milk

Beat eggs. Add sugar; beat until creamy. Stir in whipping cream and vanilla. Pour into 1-gallon container of hand-turned style ice cream freezer; fill container with milk to within 3 to 4 inches from top. Cover. Place in freezer bucket; fill bucket with alternate layers of crushed ice and half the ice amount of ice cream salt. Freeze according to freezer directions.

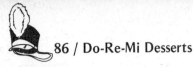

ALMOND CRUST-CHERRY CREAM PIE

1/2 c. chopped slivered almonds
Pastry for 1 9-in. pie shell
1 1/2 c. sweetened condensed milk
1/3 c. lemon juice
1 tsp. vanilla extract
1/2 tsp. almond extract
1/2 c. whipping cream, whipped
2/3 c. cherry juice
1/4 c. sugar
1 tbsp. cornstarch
3 drops of red food coloring
2 c. drained pitted sour cherries

Add almonds to pastry; roll out on floured surface to fit 9-inch pie pan. Place in pan; prick side of shell. Bake in preheated 425-degree oven for 10 to 12 minutes; let cool. Combine milk, lemon juice, vanilla and almond extracts; mix until thickened. Fold in whipped cream; spoon into cooled shell. Combine cherry juice, sugar and cornstarch in saucepan; cook over low heat, stirring constantly, until thickened and clear. Add red food coloring and cherries; spread over cream filling. Chill for 2 to 3 hours. Yield: 6 servings.

CHERRY TARTS

3/4 c. sugar
2 tbsp. cornstarch
1/2 tsp. salt
3 tbsp. orange juice
1 tbsp. lemon juice
1 c. unsweetened cherry juice
2 tbsp. butter
1 tsp. grated orange rind
4 c. red tart unsweetened cherries
9 baked tart shells

Combine sugar, cornstarch, salt and fruit juices in saucepan; cook for 5 minutes or until thickened and clear. Remove from heat; stir in butter, orange rind and cherries. Let cool. Spoon into tart shells. Top with ice cream or whipped cream, if desired.

FRESH COCONUT PIE

3 eggs
1 1/2 c. sugar
2 tbsp. flour
2 tbsp. melted butter
1 tsp. vanilla
1 fresh coconut, grated
1 1/2 c. milk
1 unbaked 9-in. pie shell

Beat eggs slightly; add sugar, flour, butter, vanilla and coconut. Stir in milk slowly, mixing well. Pour into pie shell. Bake in preheated 400-degree oven until lightly browned and center is set.

LYRICAL LIME PIE

1 9-oz. container Cool Whip
1 6-oz. can frozen limeade concentrate, thawed
1 15-oz. can sweetened condensed milk
1/2 tsp. lemon juice
2 9-in. graham cracker pie crusts

Combine Cool Whip, limeade concentrate, milk and lemon juice; spoon into crusts. Chill until cold. May add green food coloring, if desired. Will keep in refrigerator for 1 week.

ORANGE PIE OVATION

3/4 c. chopped macadamia nuts
1 1/4 c. flaked coconut
3/4 c. sugar
1/2 c. melted butter
1 3/4 c. orange juice
3 tbsp. cornstarch
2/3 c. orange marmalade
1 tbsp. vanilla extract
6 oranges

Combine macadamia nuts, coconut, 1/4 cup sugar and butter; mix well. Reserve 1/2 cup coconut mixture; press remaining mixture in pie pan to form crust. Bake in preheated 375-degree oven for 10 minutes or until browned. Combine orange juice, cornstarch, remaining 1/2 cup sugar, orange marmalade and vanilla extract in saucepan; cook over medium heat until thickened and clear, stirring constantly. Remove from heat; let cool. Peel oranges and remove membrane from slices. Line pie crust with orange slices; sprinkle reserved coconut mixture over slices. Spread filling over slices. May be topped with whipped cream, if desired.

Recipe on page 81.

PUMPKIN PIE ON PARADE

1 recipe 1-crust pie pastry
2 eggs, beaten
1 1-lb. can pumpkin
1 c. sugar
1/2 tsp. salt
1/2 tsp. cinnamon
1/2 tsp. ginger
1/4 tsp. allspice
1/8 tsp. cloves
1 3/4 c. milk
1 c. whipping cream, whipped

Roll out pastry; place in deep 9-inch pie pan. Flute pastry edge. Stir eggs into pumpkin; mix well. Combine sugar, salt and spices; stir into pumpkin mixture. Add milk gradually; stir until well mixed. Pour into pastry shell. Bake in preheated 450-degree oven for 10 minutes. Reduce oven temperature to 350 degrees; bake for 1 hour longer or until knife inserted in center comes out clean. Spread whipped cream over top of cooled pie.

MARDI GRAS PECAN PIE

2 tbsp. flour
2 tbsp. butter, melted
3 eggs, beaten
2 tsp. vanilla extract
1/8 tsp. salt
1/2 c. sugar
1 1/2 c. dark corn syrup
1 1/2 c. pecan halves
1 unbaked 9-in. pie shell

Combine flour and butter; mix until smooth. Stir in eggs. Add vanilla, salt, sugar and syrup. Sprinkle pecans in pie shell; pour syrup mixture carefully over pecans. Bake in preheated 425-degree oven for 10 minutes. Reduce oven temperature; bake for 35 minutes longer or until firm.

BANANA TURNOVERS

4 c. unsifted all-purpose flour
2 tsp. salt
1 1/3 c. shortening
4 bananas

Recipes on pages 84, 85 and 91.

8 tbsp. raisins
8 tsp. sunflower seed

Combine flour and salt in large bowl; cut in shortening until mixture resembles coarse meal. Sprinkle with 1/3 cup cold water; mix lightly with fork. Divide pastry into 8 balls. Roll out each ball of pastry on lightly floured board into 8-inch square. Peel bananas; cut into slices. Place 1/2 sliced banana on half of each square of pastry. Add 1 tablespoon raisins and 1 teaspoon sunflower seed to bananas; fold end of dough over filling to form a triangle. Seal edges. Place on ungreased baking sheet. Bake in preheated 400-degree oven for 15 to 20 minutes or until done. Remove from baking sheet; let cool slightly before serving.

Photograph for this recipe on page 70.

TCHAIKOVSKY'S CHOCOLATE PUDDING

1/3 c. cocoa
2/3 c. sugar
1/4 c. cornstarch
Dash of salt
2 c. milk
1/3 c. evaporated milk
2 egg yolks
1 tsp. vanilla extract
Whipped cream

Combine cocoa, sugar, cornstarch and salt in saucepan. Add milks and egg yolks; mix well. Cook over low heat until mixture thickens, stirring constantly. Remove from heat; stir in vanilla. Let cool. Serve with whipped cream.

SPECIAL PEACH PUDDING

4 c. chopped peeled peaches
1 2/3 c. sugar
1 c. flour
1/3 c. milk
1/3 c. butter, softened
1 egg, beaten

Cover peaches with 1 cup sugar; set aside. Combine remaining 2/3 cup sugar with remaining ingredients in bowl; mix well. Fold in peaches; pour into well-greased deep baking dish. Bake in preheated 350-degree oven for 40 minutes. May serve hot or cold with whipped cream or dessert topping.

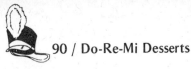

GOURMET CHEESECAKE

1 1/2 c. graham cracker crumbs
Sugar
1/2 c. melted butter
1 tbsp. cinnamon
5 eggs, separated
1 1/2 lb. cream cheese, softened
1/2 c. sifted flour
1 1/2 c. sour cream
1 1/2 tbsp. lemon juice
1 tsp. vanilla extract

Combine cracker crumbs, 3 tablespoons sugar, butter and cinnamon; mix well. Reserve part of the mixture for topping; press remaining mixture on bottom and side of large greased springform pan. Beat egg whites until frothy. Add 1/2 cup sugar gradually; beat until stiff peaks form. Combine egg yolks, 3/4 cup sugar, cream cheese, flour, sour cream, lemon juice and vanilla; beat until smooth. Fold egg whites into cheese mixture; pour into crust. Top with reserved crumb mixture. Bake in preheated 350-degree oven for 1 hour. Let cheesecake cool in oven for 1 hour. Remove from oven; let cool before serving.

LEMON LYRE DELIGHT

1 c. butter
2 c. confectioners' sugar
4 eggs, separated
Juice and grated rind of 1 lg. lemon
1 c. chopped pecans
1 tsp. vanilla extract
1 1/2 doz. ladyfingers, split

Cream butter and confectioners' sugar until fluffy; stir in well-beaten egg yolks. Add lemon juice, rind, pecans and vanilla; mix well. Fold in stiffly beaten egg whites. Line bottom of springform pan with half the ladyfingers; spread on half the filling. Add remaining ladyfingers; top with remaining filling. Refrigerate overnight. Serve with whipped cream.

Meringue will not shrink if you spread it on the pie so that it touches the crust on side and bake it in a moderate oven.

BANANA SPLIT DESSERT

2 c. crushed graham crackers
Butter
2 c. powdered sugar
1 tsp. vanilla extract
2 eggs, lightly beaten
Firm bananas
1 lg. can crushed pineapple
2 c. whipped cream
1/4 c. crushed nuts
Maraschino cherries

Combine cracker crumbs and 6 tablespoons melted butter, mixing well. Press crumb mixture into bottom of 13 x 9-inch pan. Combine 1/2 cup butter, sugar, vanilla and eggs; beat until fluffy. Spread sugar mixture over crumb layer. Slice bananas lengthwise; arrange over sugar mixture. Spoon pineapple over bananas; cover pineapple layer with whipped cream. Sprinkle with nuts; garnish with cherries. Chill for 6 hours before serving.

FABULOUS FINALE

2 c. fine vanilla wafer crumbs
1/3 c. melted butter

1/2 c. butter
1 1/2 c. sifted confectioners' sugar
2 eggs
1/4 c. sugar
3 tbsp. cocoa
1 c. heavy cream
1 c. chopped walnuts
1 ripe banana, mashed
1/4 c. sliced maraschino cherries

Mix crumbs and melted butter, reserving 2 table-spoons for top. Press remaining mixture in 1-quart refrigerator tray. Cream butter and confectioners' sugar until fluffy; add eggs, 1 at a time, beating well after each addition. Spread over crumbs. Combine sugar and cocoa. Whip cream until foamy; add cocoa mixture gradually, beating until stiff. Fold in walnuts, banana and cherries. Spread over butter mixture. Sprinkle reserved crumbs over top. Chill for 24 hours; cut into slices. Yield: 12 servings.

EGRO AMBROSIA

4 lg. navel oranges
6 tbsp. confectioners' sugar
1 c. grated coconut
3 tbsp. orange juice

Peel oranges; remove all outer membrane. Cut between membranes to remove sections. Combine with remaining ingredients; chill before serving. Yield: 3 servings.

BANANAS WITH CUSTARD SAUCE

1 tbsp. cornstarch
2 tbsp. sugar
2 1/3 c. milk
4 egg yolks, slightly beaten
1 tsp. vanilla
6 bananas

Combine cornstarch and sugar in top of double boiler; stir in milk. Place over low direct heat; cook until mixture thickens slightly, stirring constantly. Remove from heat. Stir a small amount of hot milk mixture into egg yolks; stir egg yolks into hot milk mixture. Place over boiling water; cook, stirring constantly, until mixture thickens. Remove from heat; stir in vanilla. Chill thoroughly. Peel bananas; cut into chunks. Place in serving bowl or individual dishes; pour custard sauce over bananas. Serve immediately. Yield: 6 servings.

Photograph for this recipe on page 70.

COFFEE SHAKE

1/2 c. milk
1/4 tsp. instant coffee powder
1 ripe banana, chopped
1 egg
1/4 c. crushed ice or 2 ice cubes

Combine all ingredients in electric blender container. Cover; process at high speed until foamy. Yield: 1 serving.

Photograph for this recipe on page 70.

TOUCHDOWN PUNCH

4 c. Ocean Spray cranberry juice cocktail
4 c. grapefruit juice
2 12-oz. cans apricot nectar
2 cinnamon sticks
12 whole cloves
Lemon slices

Combine all ingredients except lemon slices in saucepan. Bring to a boil; simmer for 5 minutes. Remove spices; pour into mugs. Garnish with lemon slices. Hot punch may be poured into thermos jug and taken to the football game. Yield: 12 servings.

Photograph for this recipe on page 28.

PEPPERMINT FLOAT

2 tbsp. finely crushed peppermint candy
1 qt. peppermint ice cream
4 c. milk

Combine candy, 1 pint softened ice cream and milk in large mixing bowl; beat at low speed of electric mixer until slushy. Pour into chilled glasses; top each glass with a scoop of ice cream. Garnish with crushed candy, if desired.

Photograph for this recipe on page 88.

Volume Recipes

Planning the menu and preparing the food for a crowd — cooks have been doing this for hundreds of years, yet it never fails to cause the unexperienced cook moments of anxiety. What foods are suitable for large crowds? How much of all the ingredients will I have to buy? What foods will be as easy to prepare as they are delicious? Thankfully, because feeding large groups of people has long been a part of our heritage, plenty of good large-quantity recipes have been developed.

Potato salad and fried chicken, or hot dogs, baked beans and coleslaw have always been the favorites for large picnics and informal gatherings. For an awards dinner or party, though, you will want to offer a menu that everyone will remember for a long time. *Crowd-Pleasing Shrimp Creole* or *Banquet Chicken a la King* are first-rate entrees. Then, to round out the meal with a vegetable and a salad, try *Cheesy Green Bean Casserole* or *Vegetable Medley*, and *Reception Fruit Salad* or *Timpani Tossed Salad*. A meal like this may deserve a special award of its own!

The band members and cheering squad offer these recipes to you with confidence — and in hopes that some of the dishes will be included at their next banquet or picnic!

BIG BATCH FROZEN SALAD

4   1-lb. 4-oz. cans crushed pineapple
2   1-lb. cans sliced peaches
2 c. fresh white seedless grapes, halved
1 1/2 c. maraschino cherries, cut in eighths
1/2 lb. marshmallows, quartered
2 tsp. chopped crystallized ginger
1 env. unflavored gelatin
1/4 c. cold water
1 c. orange juice
1/4 c. lemon juice
2 1/2 c. sugar
1/2 tsp. salt
2 c. coarsely chopped pecans
2 qt. heavy cream, whipped
2 c. mayonnaise

Drain fruits, reserving 1 1/2 cups pineapple juice. Cut peaches in 1/2-inch cubes. Combine fruits, marshmallows and ginger. Soften gelatin in cold water. Bring pineapple juice to a boil; add gelatin, stirring until dissolved. Add orange juice, lemon juice, sugar and salt. Chill until thickened. Add fruit mixture and pecans; fold in whipped cream and mayonnaise. Spoon into nine 1-quart cylinder cartons; cover. Freeze. Remove from freezer; thaw enough to slip from cartons. Cut in 1-inch slices. Serve salad on lettuce; garnish with cherries. Yield: 65 servings.

FRUIT SALAD BALLAD

12 eggs, beaten
3 c. sugar
3 c. vinegar
1 1/4 c. butter
1 qt. cream, whipped
12 lb. seedless green grapes
20   15-oz. cans pineapple tidbits, drained
4 pkg. miniature marshmallows

Combine eggs, sugar and vinegar in large saucepan; cook, stirring constantly, until thick. Add butter; stir until butter is melted. Cool. Fold in whipped cream. Blend in grapes, pineapple and marshmallows. Chill for several hours. Yield: 75 servings.

RECEPTION FRUIT SALAD

12 oranges, peeled and sectioned
2 lg. cans pineapple chunks, drained
2 lg. cans sliced peaches, drained
1 lb. seedless white grapes
4 bananas, sliced
1 watermelon
1 cantaloupe
1 honeydew melon

Chill all fruits before using. Cut watermelon, cantaloupe and honeydew melon into balls or cubes. Combine all ingredients just before serving. Serve with powdered sugar. Yield: 50 servings.

CHICKEN SALAD STRUT

2 lg. chickens, cooked
1/4 c. salad oil
1/4 c. orange juice
1/4 c. vinegar
2 tsp. salt
3 c. mandarin orange sections
3 c. pineapple tidbits
3 c. green grapes
2 c. slivered almonds, toasted
3 c. diced celery
2 1/2 c. rice, cooked and cooled
1 qt. mayonnaise

Remove chicken from bones; dice. Combine oil, orange juice, vinegar and salt; add to chicken. Marinate in refrigerator for several hours, stirring occasionally. Add orange sections, pineapple, grapes, almonds, celery and rice; toss with mayonnaise. Refrigerate until ready to serve. Yield: 25 servings.

POTATO SALAD FOR FIFTY

2 1/2 c. French dressing
15 lb. potatoes, peeled, cubed and cooked
1/4 c. salt
1/2 c. vinegar or pickle juice
20 hard-boiled eggs, diced
1 1/2 qt. mayonnaise
3/4 c. minced onion
1/3 c. prepared mustard
2 tbsp. celery seed
4 c. chopped celery
1 3/4 c. sliced stuffed olives

Add French dressing to potatoes; marinate for 2 hours. Add remaining ingredients; mix well. Chill thoroughly. Yield: 50 servings.

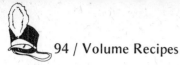

CHEERLEADER'S CHICKEN SALAD

4   14 1/4-oz. cans chicken, drained and
  chopped
12 hard-cooked eggs, chopped
4 c. chopped celery
3 1/4 c. sweet pickle relish
36 crackers, coarsely crushed
Salad dressing

Combine first 5 ingredients; stir in enough salad dressing to moisten. Yield: 40 servings.

AROUND-THE-CLOCK BEAN SALAD

2 No. 303 cans kidney beans
2 No. 303 cans green beans
2 No. 303 cans yellow wax beans
2 No. 303 cans sm. lima beans
2 No. 303 cans bean sprouts
1 c. vinegar
1 c. oil
Garlic salt to taste
1 c. sugar
1 c. chopped green pepper
1 c. chopped celery
1 c. chopped onion

Drain kidney beans and rinse. Drain remaining beans. Combine all ingredients. Refrigerate overnight. Yield: 35 servings.

TIMPANI TOSSED SALAD

6 heads lettuce
2 pkg. fresh spinach, washed and stemmed
3 bunches radishes, sliced
3 bunches green onions, sliced
3 carrots, shredded

Tear lettuce and spinach into desired size pieces. Add remaining ingredients. Toss lightly. Serve with favorite dressing. Yield: 100 servings.

KETTLEDRUM CAMP STEW

4 lb. beef
4 lb. potatoes
4 lb. onions
4 cans tomatoes
4 cans cream-style corn
4 cans baby lima beans
2 bottles catsup
1 tbsp. prepared mustard
1 1/2 lemons, cut up
1/2 c. Worcestershire sauce
Salt and pepper to taste

Cook beef in boiling, salted water until done. Remove beef from broth; set aside to cool. Reserve broth. Peel and dice potatoes and onions; place in large kettle. Add tomatoes, corn, beans, catsup, mustard, lemons and Worcestershire sauce. Remove beef from bones; cut into large pieces. Add to potato mixture. Stir in beef broth; season with salt and pepper. Cook, stirring frequently, for about 2 hours or until done. Other meats may be substituted for beef. Stew may be frozen.

SPECIAL OCCASION BEEF AU JUS

1   20-lb. standing rib of beef

Let beef stand to room temperature before roasting. Place fat side up on rack in shallow baking pan. Insert meat thermometer so tip will be in center of roast. Bake in preheated 325-degree oven to desired doneness, allowing 18 to 20 minutes per pound for rare, 22 minutes per pound for medium or 27 minutes per pound for well-done beef. Let beef stand in warm place for 20 minutes before carving.

Photograph for this recipe on page 92.

JOHNNY MARZETTI

2 eggs, beaten
1 tsp. salt
1/4 c. cream
2 c. (about) sifted flour
3 lb. hamburger
2 lb. bulk sausage
2 sm. onions, chopped
2   1-lb. 4-oz. cans corn
2   1-lb. 4-oz. cans peas, drained
Herb seasoning to taste (opt.)
Thyme to taste (opt.)
1 lb. Longhorn cheese, grated
1/4 lb. sharp cheese, grated
Salt and pepper to taste

Combine eggs, salt and cream in bowl; stir in enough flour to make stiff dough. Roll out very thin on floured surface; let rest for 20 minutes. Roll as for jelly roll; cut into 1/2-inch thick slices. Cook dry noodles in boiling, salted water until tender. Drain; reserve liquid. Cook hamburger, sausage and onions in large skillet until onions are tender. Mix with noodles and remaining ingredients; stir in enough reserved liquid to moisten. Place in greased casseroles. Bake in preheated 325-degree oven for 1 hour or until heated through. Yield: 50 servings.

SUPER SPAGHETTI AND MEATBALLS

    10 lb. ground beef
    6 c. fine dry bread crumbs
    5 tsp. garlic salt
    12 eggs
    Salt
    2 1/2 tsp. pepper
    1 1/4 c. olive oil
    5 c. tomato sauce
    4 1/2 qt. canned tomatoes
    3 cloves of garlic, minced
    1 1/4 c. finely chopped onions
    2 1/2 tsp. oregano
    5 lb. spaghetti

Combine beef, bread crumbs, garlic salt, eggs, 5 teaspoons salt and 1 1/4 teaspoons pepper; mix well. Shape into 1-inch balls. Cook in oil until lightly browned on all sides. Place tomato sauce, tomatoes, garlic, onions, 4 teaspoons salt, remaining 1 1/4 teaspoons pepper and oregano in Dutch oven; cover. Cook over low heat for 1 hour, stirring occasionally. Add meatballs; simmer for 30 minutes longer. Add spaghetti to 7 1/2 gallons rapidly boiling salted water in large kettle. Cook, partially covered, until tender, stirring occasionally; drain. Serve meatballs and sauce over spaghetti. Yield: 50 servings.

SLOPPY JOES FOR A CROWD

    15 lb. ground beef
    3 lb. onions, chopped
    1 1/2 bottles catsup
    1/2 c. prepared mustard
    5 cans chicken gumbo soup
    10 cans tomato soup
    1 c. chopped celery

Cook ground beef until brown. Mix ground beef, onions, catsup, mustard, soups and celery in large kettle; bring to a boil. Reduce heat; simmer for at least 2 hours, stirring frequently. Serve on buns.

COUNTRY KITCHEN HAM CASSEROLE

    2 12-oz. packages noodles, cooked
    3 lb. cooked ham, cubed
    5 cans green peas, drained
    5 cans cream of mushroom soup
    12 oz. sharp Cheddar cheese, diced
    3 to 4 c. milk
    3 eggs, beaten
    1 sm. onion, diced (opt.)
    Salt and pepper to taste
    Crushed potato chips

Combine all ingredients except potato chips; place in casseroles. Cover with potato chips. Bake in preheated 350-degree oven for 40 minutes. Yield: 25 servings.

Remember the first rule of carving . . . cut across the grain.

MARCHERS BARBECUED SPARERIBS

    20 lb. country-style spareribs
    1/4 c. shortening
    3 c. catsup
    3 c. water
    1/2 c. vinegar
    4 tsp. chili powder
    1/4 c. Worcestershire sauce
    1/4 c. salt
    1/2 tsp. cayenne pepper
    4 tsp. paprika
    2 tsp. pepper
    1/2 c. (packed) brown sugar

Brown spareribs in melted shortening; cover bottom of roaster pan with ribs. Combine remaining ingredients for sauce; cover ribs with layer of sauce. Layer remaining ribs in pan, covering each layer with sauce. Cover. Bake in preheated 300-degree oven for about 2 hours or until ribs are tender. Yield: 30 servings.

BANQUET CHICKEN a la KING

    8 3-lb. fryers, disjointed
    Salt and pepper to taste
    Paprika to taste
    1 c. butter
    1 c. flour
    6 c. milk
    2 cans sliced mushrooms, drained
    1 can pimento strips, drained
    3 green peppers, chopped and cooked
    8 hard-cooked eggs, chopped

Season chicken with salt, pepper and paprika; cook in simmering water until tender. Drain chicken; cool. Reserve broth. Remove chicken from bones; cut into small pieces. Melt butter in large saucepan; stir in flour until smooth. Add milk gradually, stirring constantly. Add 2 cups reserved chicken broth; cook, stirring, until thickened. Stir in chicken, mushrooms, pimento, green peppers, eggs, salt and pepper; heat through. Serve in patty shells or over toast. Yield: 35-40 servings.

SCALLOPED CHICKEN CONCERT

    2 c. butter or margarine
    3 c. flour
    1/2 tsp. celery salt
    1/2 tsp. nutmeg
    1/2 tsp. poultry seasoning
    16 c. chicken stock
    4 c. cream
    20 c. cooked diced chicken or turkey
    8 c. fine dry bread crumbs

Melt butter in large saucepan; blend in flour and seasonings. Mix chicken stock with cream; stir into flour mixture slowly. Cook until thick and smooth, stirring constantly. Place alternate layers of chicken, sauce and bread crumbs in 2 greased 12 x 20-inch baking pans; dot with additional butter. Bake in preheated 350-degree oven for 20 to 30 minutes or until bubbly. One 5-pound chicken yields 4 cups cooked, diced chicken. Yield: 50 servings.

CHICKEN ALMOND

    9 whole chicken breasts
    5 c. chopped celery
    5 c. chopped onions
    3 lb. bulk pork sausage
    1 lg. package slivered almonds
    5 c. brown rice
    5 c. mushroom stems and pieces
    Salt and pepper to taste

Cook chicken in boiling, salted water until tender. Drain chicken; reserve broth. Cool chicken. Remove chicken from bones; cut into bite-sized pieces. Saute celery, onions and sausage in skillet until onions are tender; drain off excess fat. Place in large bowl. Add enough water to reserved broth to make 7 1/2 cups liquid; pour over sausage mixture. Add chicken, almonds, rice, mushrooms, salt and pepper; mix well. Place in large casseroles; cover. Bake in preheated 350-degree oven for 1 hour and 30 minutes or until done, adding boiling water, if needed. Yield: 50 servings.

CROWD-PLEASING SHRIMP CREOLE

    2 c. chopped onions
    4 cloves of garlic
    2 c. diced celery
    1 c. diced green pepper
    1/2 c. olive oil
    10 c. canned tomatoes
    4 bay leaves
    3 tbsp. salt
    1/4 c. chopped parsley
    2 tbsp. cornstarch
    8 lb. cooked shrimp

Saute onions, garlic, celery and green pepper in olive oil in large skillet until tender, but not brown. Add remaining ingredients except cornstarch and shrimp; cook over low heat until most of the moisture has evaporated. Remove garlic. Mix cornstarch with 1/4 cup water until smooth; stir into tomato mixture. Add shrimp; cook for 10 minutes longer. Serve over rice. Yield: 25 servings.

HALIBUT LUNCHEON CASSEROLE

    6 lb. halibut fillets
    5 tbsp. salt
    1 1/2 c. chopped green pepper
    3 c. chopped celery
    3 c. chopped onions
    1 c. butter
    2 qt. cooked 1/2-in. wide noodles

1/4 c. chopped pimento
6 hard-cooked eggs, chopped
1 c. flour
1 tbsp. paprika
6 c. milk
6 c. grated sharp Cheddar cheese
1 1/2 c. mayonnaise
Buttered bread crumbs

Place halibut in large saucepan; cover with cold water. Add 2 tablespoons salt; cook over medium heat until water comes to a boil or halibut turns white. Remove from heat; drain. Cut halibut into bite-sized pieces. Saute green pepper, celery and onions in 1/2 cup butter until tender; mix with halibut. Stir in noodles, pimento and eggs. Melt remaining 1/2 cup butter in saucepan; stir in flour, remaining 3 tablespoons salt and paprika until smooth. Add milk slowly; cook, stirring constantly, until thickened. Add 4 cups cheese; stir until melted. Add to halibut mixture; mix well. Stir in mayonnaise; place in 2 greased 9 x 13-inch baking pans. Cover with bread crumbs; sprinkle with remaining cheese. Bake in preheated 350-degree oven for 30 to 35 minutes. Other white fish may be used instead of halibut. Yield: 35 servings.

GREEN RICE

2 lg. packages frozen chopped broccoli
2 c. rice
1 c. chopped onions
1 c. chopped celery
1/2 c. margarine
2 cans cream of celery soup
1 soup can water
2 c. grated Cheddar cheese

Cook broccoli and rice separately according to package directions. Drain broccoli well. Saute onions and celery in margarine until tender; stir in soup and water. Add rice, broccoli and cheese; mix well. Turn into 2 large casseroles. Bake in preheated 350-degree oven for 25 minutes. Yield: 20 servings.

TEXAS-STYLE BEANS

4 1-lb. 13-oz. cans pork and beans
1 c. catsup
1/4 c. prepared mustard
1/4 c. Worcestershire sauce

Dash of cayenne pepper (opt.)
2 tbsp. horseradish
1/2 c. (packed) brown sugar
1 tsp. minced garlic
1 tsp. chili powder
1/4 c. celery seed
1/4 c. molasses
12 slices thick bacon, cut into thirds

Mix all ingredients except bacon; place in 2 large casseroles. Bake in preheated 350-degree oven for about 1 hour. Cook bacon in skillet until golden brown. Press 18 bacon pieces into beans in each casserole; bake until beans are brown. Yield: 24 servings.

CHEESY GREEN BEAN CASSEROLE

1 lb. sliced mushrooms
1 lg. onion, sliced
1 c. butter
1/2 c. flour
6 c. milk
1 lb. Cheddar cheese, grated
1/4 tsp. Tabasco sauce
2 tsp. salt
1/2 tsp. pepper
1 tbsp. soy sauce
6 pkg. frozen green beans
2 5-oz. cans water chestnuts
1 c. slivered almonds

Saute mushrooms and onion in butter until tender. Add flour; mix well. Add milk; cook, stirring, until smooth. Add cheese, Tabasco sauce, salt, pepper and soy sauce; simmer, stirring, until cheese melts. Cook beans according to package directions; drain. Drain water chestnuts; slice. Mix beans and water chestnuts with mushroom mixture; pour into 2 large casseroles. Sprinkle almonds over top. Bake in preheated 375-degree oven for 30 minutes. Yield: 20 servings.

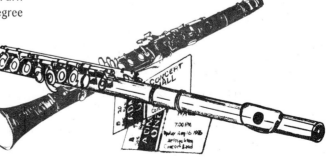

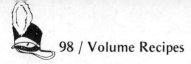

SCALLOPED POTATOES WITH CHEESE SAUCE

1 c. margarine
1 c. flour
3 qt. milk
1 tbsp. salt
1 lb. grated cheese
2 tsp. prepared mustard
Dash of paprika
10 lb. potatoes, peeled, sliced and cooked

Melt margarine in large saucepan; stir in flour. Add milk gradually; cook, stirring constantly, until thickened. Add salt, cheese, mustard and paprika; stir until cheese is melted. Place alternate layers of potatoes and cheese sauce in large, greased casserole. Bake in preheated 350-degree oven until bubbly. Yield: 25 servings.

SQUASH CASSEROLE

6 lb. yellow squash, sliced
4 onions, chopped
4 carrots, sliced
2 sm. jars pimentos
4 cans cream of chicken soup
2 cartons sour cream
1 c. melted butter
2 pkg. corn bread stuffing mix

Cook squash, onions and carrots together in salted water to cover until tender; drain well. Drain pimentos; chop. Add soup, sour cream and pimentos to squash mixture; mix well. Mix butter and stuffing mix. Spread half the stuffing mixture in 2 greased casseroles; add squash mixture. Cover with remaining stuffing mixture. Bake in preheated 375-degree oven for 45 minutes. Yield: 24 servings.

VEGETABLE MEDLEY

4 c. diagonally cut celery
4 c. canned or frozen green beans
4 c. sliced carrots
3 c. onions, sliced in rings
3 c. diced green peppers
4 c. canned or fresh tomatoes
6 tbsp. tapioca
2 tbsp. sugar
1/2 c. butter
1 tsp. pepper

Combine all ingredients in large bowl; place in 2 large casseroles. Cover. Bake in preheated 350-degree oven for about 1 hour and 30 minutes or until vegetables are tender. Yield: 20-24 servings.

SWEET POTATO CASSEROLE

20 lb. sweet potatoes, cooked
12 c. sugar
1 1/2 lb. soft butter
4 tsp. baking powder
10 eggs
2 lg. cans crushed pineapple, undrained
3 cans flaked coconut

Place potatoes, sugar, butter, baking powder and eggs in large mixing bowl; beat with electric mixer until mixed. Stir in pineapple. Pour into 2 large baking dishes. Bake in preheated 400-degree oven for about 20 minutes. Sprinkle with coconut; bake until lightly browned. Yield: 90 servings.

PETITS FOURS

1/4 c. butter
1/4 c. shortening
1 1/4 c. sugar
1/2 tsp. vanilla extract
1/4 tsp. almond extract
2 c. cake flour
1/4 tsp. salt
3 tsp. baking powder
3/4 c. milk
3/4 c. egg whites
Confectioners' sugar frosting

Cream butter, shortening and 1 cup sugar in bowl; stir in extracts. Sift flour, salt and baking powder together; add to creamed mixture alternately with milk. Beat egg whites until frothy; beat until stiff peaks form, adding remaining 1/4 cup sugar gradually. Fold into batter; pour into 2 waxed paper-lined jelly roll pans with 1-inch sides. Bake in preheated 350-degree oven for about 20 minutes or until done. Cut into squares, ovals or triangles; spread frosting over tops and sides of cake pieces.

Index

PHOTOGRAPH RECIPES

PHOTOGRAPHY CREDITS: National Livestock and Meat Board; Tuna Research Foundation; United Fresh Fruit and Vegetable Association; Sterno, Inc.; The McIlhenny Company; Accent International; The Banana Bunch; Florida Department of Citrus; United Dairy Industry Association; EL MOLINO — Cara Coa Brand; DIAMOND Walnut Growers, Inc.; Olive Administrative Committee; Ocean Spray Cranberries, Inc.; Pineapple Growers Association; California Raisin Advisory Board; National Macaroni Institute; Standard Brands Products: Fleischmann's Yeast, Fleischmann's Margarine; National Dairy Council; California Beef Council.

FAVORITE RECIPES® PRESENTS

Kitchen Auditions

A Cookbook for Bands and Cheering Squads

Order Form 60790

PLEASE SEND ME THE FOLLOWING BOOKS:
(NOTE: School Bands & Cheering Squads
should request special discount order forms.)

Quan.	Cookbook Title	Item No.	Price Each	Total
	"KITCHEN AUDITIONS"	136001	$3.50	

Name

Address

City   State   Zip

☐ Please Bill Me — Plus Postage and Handling.

☐ Enclosed is payment for full amount. No charge for postage and handling.

MAIL TO: FAVORITE RECIPES PRESS • ORDER PROCESSING
P.O. BOX 2020 • LATHAM, NEW YORK 12111

Order Form 60790

PLEASE SEND ME THE FOLLOWING BOOKS:
(NOTE: School Bands & Cheering Squads
should request special discount order forms.)

Quan.	Cookbook Title	Item No.	Price Each	Total
	"KITCHEN AUDITIONS"	136001	$3.50	

Name

Address

City   State   Zip

☐ Please Bill Me — Plus Postage and Handling.

☐ Enclosed is payment for full amount. No charge for postage and handling.

MAIL TO: FAVORITE RECIPES PRESS • ORDER PROCESSING
P.O. BOX 2020 • LATHAM, NEW YORK 12111

Order Form 60790

PLEASE SEND ME THE FOLLOWING BOOKS:
(NOTE: School Bands & Cheering Squads
should request special discount order forms.)

Quan.	Cookbook Title	Item No.	Price Each	Total
	"KITCHEN AUDITIONS"	136001	$3.50	

Name

Address

City   State   Zip

☐ Please Bill Me — Plus Postage and Handling.

☐ Enclosed is payment for full amount. No charge for postage and handling.

MAIL TO: FAVORITE RECIPES PRESS • ORDER PROCESSING
P.O. BOX 2020 • LATHAM, NEW YORK 12111